Charles Fleming Embree

For the love of Tonita & other tales of the mesas

Charles Fleming Embree

For the love of Tonita & other tales of the mesas

ISBN/EAN: 9783743322110

Manufactured in Europe, USA, Canada, Australia, Japa

Cover: Foto ©Thomas Meinert / pixelio.de

Manufactured and distributed by brebook publishing software
(www.brebook.com)

Charles Fleming Embree

For the love of Tonita & other tales of the mesas

The Contents

FOR THE LOVE OF TONITA

❦

THE sun shone on the mesas far to the east and the broad valley stretching between them, on the little stream that sparkled in its light, on the old adobe fort with its surrounding huts, and on the three mountains far to the left whence the stream had come. The fort, a hollow square lacking the fourth side, comprised numerous adobe dwellings joined into continuous walls; some in ruins, but the mere suggestions of former houses, with the adobes fallen in heaps about their bases; and some still habitable. The stream, scarcely two yards in width, ran on the outer side of the western wall, and beyond it, under the rise of the trail, a few straggling huts stood among low willows.

Out of the largest house of the eastern wall, its door facing within the square,

that shone in the doorway, and faced
Tonita. Her face was the swarthy one
of the Mexican, and she answered the
girl's pure Spanish in the Mexican dia-
lect. She puffed a little at her cigarette,
gave a grunt of disgust, and said:

" What is to be done with her? I have
tried, the old Don has tried, Carlota has
tried. Pah! I have smoked nine cigarettes in thinking it out, and it is not
thought out. She loves you, Tonita,
more than us all, more than me, her
mother. You go. Pah! it will do no
good, but you go."

Noiselessly Tonita entered the next
room, the only other one. One window
let in meager light. There were two
chairs, and a bed against the wall, and a
rude table near the window. A rear door
open gave view between some straggling
willows, across the plain, lit with the late
afternoon sun. There was a little sob
from near the door as she entered, and a
bundle of white upon the floor quivered
somewhat. Tonita closed the door behind her.

" Ines? " she said.

There was another sob from the bundle on the floor.

"Why, Ines,—my blessed Ines," said Tonita, her clear voice full of compassion, "it is Tonita. Look at me; talk to me!"

She spoke as though to a child she loved. She stood for a second above the bundle on the floor, then suddenly stooped beside it, half kneeling. Her white face seemed whiter in the half-light of the room, and her eyes as black as the shadows beneath the table and the chairs. She put her arms about the bundle of white.

"You will come — for me, Ines?"

With a greater sob Ines only drew herself closer.

"My beautiful Ines, what is it — tell me! Only the thing Juan said to you? It was nothing. Juan is thoughtless, he meant nothing. Come, I cannot bear for you to be thus."

"O, Tonita — it is not that alone!" The words were mingled with many sobs. "Only—it made me think it all again,— all that has made me wretched so many times. And now when I wanted to forget it,— now, of all times. O, Tonita,

Tonita! why was I not like you?"

"I have tried so much, Ines," said Tonita, "to keep you from thinking so. There is no need to say it all again. Is it not enough that I, Tonita, who have always called you sister, tell you you think wrongly? It is enough that I love you, that we all love you, that to us you are the same."

"I know, I know. Only — for him."

Tonita caught her breath a little, and looked at the willows without, and for a moment said nothing. Then, pityingly, again she turned her eyes upon the black hair against her arm.

"He has told you — there is no difference to him."

"But after a time — not now, I know. He will see it more plainly. Already it seems he watches you and Carlota, and maybe — maybe — what if he forget me? Juan says I am only a Mexican. He says Ramon will curse in me the Indian blood. He is cruel, and points me out my dark face and the hateful straight hair. He says that I want to marry Ramon because he is all Spanish; that I want to raise myself above Juan and my mother. Oh! I cannot bear it! It is lies — lies — lies! Tonita, you know — you know that it is because I love him; that I loved him when first he came and said he was your cousin, when first we went down the stream together — there where the verbenas grew, and the sun shone on the rocks, and I pointed out the mountains to him, and sang. You know it was like this ever since, just burning me up, as though it will kill me; that I cannot sleep for thinking of him; that I cannot eat, nor talk, nor sing, when he is away; that I would die for him — die for him!"

The words came hot and passionately, and the form trembled against Tonita's arm. Ines suddenly threw back her head, her face flushed, and the tears in her eyes.

"Tell me!" she cried, looking into Tonita's face; "is it so plain? Am I terrible with it? Oh! what is it that makes the difference so? Is it this that I feel? Is it the heat that comes all over me and rushes to my temples, and fills my brain, and throbs, throbs, throbs, till I must cry out? If it were not for you — you and

him—I feel sometimes it would show itself indeed; that I could terrify Juan with
it out of desperation, prove to him all too
well that he is right; that I cannot get the
wild blood out. But for you and him I am
content. I feel only that I am wicked to
be unhappy. Tonita, I am enough like
you? Say I am!"

"Ines! Ines! you must not, must not
talk so. Why, you are wrong to him to
doubt it. Let yourself be once at rest.
Do not listen to Juan. Ramon loves you
—he has told you so. What else do you
want?"

Ines arose and stood by the door and
looked out, and Tonita stood beside her.
The former was very young, scarcely more
than seventeen. Her face was dark, with
a rich red glow in the delicate skin, a complexion showing more of the blood of
Spain than the wilder element she hated.
The hair hung loose about her shoulders,
straight and black.

"When I think of that alone, it is all
right," she said. "Yet Juan says he will
learn the difference and hate me."

Tonita was silent. She turned her face

to the shadow, but the blood was in her cheeks. The quick instinct of the Mexican seized upon the silence instantly.

" You say nothing ! " she said, catching Tonita's hand. " It is not true—say it is not true ! Oh ! " with a wild motion of her hands above her head, " it will kill me ! I cannot bear it ! See—here on the table is the knife Juan gave me. Sometimes I think I will take it up like this — see ! If he did not love me, Tonita, I would kill myself ! It is all I have ! "

" Ines ! " cried the Spaniard, seizing the knife and placing it on the table again. She caught the girl in her arms and held her quiet against her breast, till the passionate heart found vent again in sobs. Still, Tonita looked away into the sunlight. There was the shadow of sorrow in her eyes, and the blood still throbbed in her cheeks. The head upon her shoulder had almost ceased to tremble with the sobs, when she at last spoke.

" Listen, Ines. Juan is wrong, that he makes you think of it always. Ramon has told you he loves you. You know that you love him. You have only to risk,

then, what we all must risk. You want
to show yourself equal to his race. This
is the way to do it: Keep down this hot,
hot blood of yours, little one, — for my
sake, then, if for nothing else, keep it
down. Then take what comes to you in
calmness. Trust it all, Ines. Trust to
us who love you. The blood that makes
you wild and restless, that is what we love;
that is what makes you true; that is what
won Ramon. Do not be ashamed of it,
only keep it in bounds. You will make
him love you the more."

"You are better to me than is any one
else," cried the girl. "I owe it all to you.
Since first your padre brought us here, and
made me come and be your friend, and
taught me so much I never knew before;
since then you have always been with me,
loved me, made me so different. Yes, for
you I will try."

"Then come; you are better now. It is
all right. Come with me. This last supper
we want you with us. You will come?"

"Will Ramon be there?"

"He has come already. He was putting away his horse. You will come?"

"Yes—now I will come."

They went out together and crossed the stream. When they had gone, the old woman in the next room arose and went to the front door and grunted a little to herself and puffed at her cigarette.

"What can be made out of a girl like that?" she said. "What is she thinking about all the time? I cannot manage her —pah! my talk is like rain to the ducks. What is in Tonita that she makes her listen?"

Juan came tramping through the willows with a gun across his shoulder. He had stood for a moment at the stream and watched the girls disappear. He approached his mother with a scowl upon his face. His features were coarse and swarthy. At present there was not much above the brute showing in them. He was thick-set and of medium height.

"That is it," he said gruffly, in Mexican, passing his mother and setting down his gun in the corner. "That is it. What can you make out of her but that she is proud? She sits all day and pouts, only that they may come and coax her and at last almost carry her, so that we cannot say she left us of her own accord."

"Be still!" cried his mother sharply, her wrinkled face screwed into an expression of displeasure, and her sharp black eyes turning upon him. "It is you who make trouble, with your talk. You want your old mother to die without seeing her daughter married. Yes — you want us to lie and rot, to grind, and grind, and grind!"

Juan threw his cartridges angrily on the narrow bed that stood against the wall.

"What right has she to set herself above us all and give herself airs?" he said.

"There you are now," chimed in his mother, "at it again! You are selfish, you are hateful to your own blood. It is a fine thing—ah! it is a fine thing that she has taken Ramon. Why, I look out at the mesas and the cattle, and they look different since I know she has got Ramon. Pah! you want to crawl the ground forever. Why — she is a lady now; she is up with the best of them; she will have money, money. It was her good looks that did it. She

got them from me. There was n't a one
of them could hold a face to me when I
was young. I was a beauty. If it is all
wrinkled up now, it was a face for the best
of them. It is what she deserves!"

The old Mexican stepped unsteadily to
the door and back again as she talked,
puffing at her cigarette, motioning excitedly with her hands, and calling into
play the muscles of her face.

"But it is this, mother," said Juan, stopping in front of her. "It is spoiling it all
for me. You know I have got work at
Taos, better than any of this work. You
know I am going almost at once, as soon
as this wedding is out of the way. You
know I had planned that you and Ines go
with me and keep the house, that I would
not have to pay others, for the house will
come with the work if I have you to keep
it. And I would take you and her, and we
would live the way I want to live, where
there are more people than here in this lost
place, with nothing but cattle and mesas
yonder and mountains back here. And
now you refuse. You say that because
Ines stays here, you stay here. I have to

go by myself; I have to live in the hut alone; I have to cook alone; or I must go and pay my wages for some one else or get myself married to some slovenly woman in Taos. It is selfish in you both. It is because she is proud and thinks she is better than I."

"Dios! you foolish child! All for yourself, your hut, your work, your wages, your cooking. Pah! always are they just to sit on the dirt floor and work for you, the women? That is how fine a young man you are! You are no son of mine."

"But I do n't like this marriage. I do n't like this Ramon with his long fingers."

"You do n't like your own cooking, better say — and well enough." She laughed a long, croaking laugh. "No more do the rest of us. It is not the best kind. But this marriage shall be. She shall be as good as the next one. Tonita says she is already, and Tonita is right."

Juan tramped through the rear room, and went sullenly about some work behind the hut.

Meanwhile the two girls had entered the house that faced within the square of the fort. It was a long, low adobe structure, set in among the others that formed the wall. Its rooms were large, and furnished with much more refinement than those of the huts. The smooth floors of hard earth were, in the main, covered with carpets; the great adobe fireplaces sparkled with burning pine, for the evening had come, and a fresher breeze from the mountains. There were some books about, an old guitar in a corner, old portraits on the walls, and other reminders of Spanish luxury. The house, together with a high adobe wall to the rear, surrounded a small placita, or inner court. Across this the light from the dining-room shone brightly. This was the abode of Don Carlos, the old Spaniard, Tonita's father. He was a sort of acknowledged lord of the fort and its minute settlement, owner of the grazing-land about, and benefactor to the Mexicans.

The family was seated about the dining-table, talking volubly in Spanish, gesticulating at times, answering the light of the lamps with the sparkle of black Spanish eyes. Ines sat next to Tonita. The impetuous child had wholly changed her mood. She was as merry, as irrepressible, as a frolicsome kitten. Her high-strung nature treated her always thus, bandying her about among different moods. Don Carlos, at the head of the table, cast his keen eyes at her in silent approval. He had always loved this wayward child, scarcely second to Tonita here on his left or Carlota on his right.

His was a striking face; his features delicate, yet firm and worn with hardships uncounted; his beard gray, showing his age scarcely less than did his bent form when he walked; his high forehead still white where the hair joined it. His wife, at the foot of the table, was liveliest of them all. Her cheeks were full, her complexion dark, and her eyes of a brilliancy that it would take many years yet to dim. Her expression showed a mixture of enjoyment and benevolence. A shade passed over her face at times as she glanced at Tonita. Tonita ate but little, busying herself in her care for Ines, answering the girl's many questions, seeing that she wanted nothing. She did not look across the table.

Beside Carlota, across the table, sat Ramon. He was a tall, broad-shouldered young Spaniard, noticeable in that his hair was lighter than that of most Spaniards. His complexion, too, like Tonita's, was peculiarly white. The bronze of the sun and the wind could not cover it up. His face was a strong one and his eyes sparkling. He, too, sat silent.

"Ramon, Ramon," said the Señora, Tonita's mother, turning her face quickly toward him, "why do you not speak? You are eating almost nothing at all. Tut, tut, boy! and to-morrow your wedding-day! Why, look at Ines there. The little kitten is as frisky as an antelope on the mesas. Ah, such eyes, Ramon! See her blush when I say it; look at the blood come up—up—up—ah!" with a peal of laughter from them all as they watched the color throbbing in Ines's cheeks; "what did I say? That blush is yours, Ramon! Look at the smile, too! that little lower lip of hers, which points so bewitchingly in the middle. Ramon, Ramon! you see all this, and you are silent!"

"Do n't you see, Señora," said Ramon, his face lighting up to some degree, "do n't you see it is because I am just looking,—just sitting looking? What more could a fellow do? Who could talk with it just overpowering him?"

"Besides," chimed in Carlota, a girl of gentle eyes and rich, dark complexion, "Ines is doing it all; and Papa there feeding her all the time, too, till one would think she would choke. Nevertheless she talks for us all. Is it not so, Ines?"

"O," said Ines, pointing her little lip and putting on a mock pout, "you all tease me,—O, I am so bothered with you all! Look at you all now, just stare at me so till I feel the blood in me all running up into my cheeks, and I try to put it down, and it runs up the more, till it blushes itself into a big laugh and just will come out, and you say I am silly! I won't look at you,—there now! See, here are three leaves I pulled from the willows. One of them I wore on my

heart. That was for—well," with a blush
and the sweetest of sweet laughter, and
her big black eyes sweeping the circle of
them and sparkling, " well—for *some*body.
The next one I had at my throat, for Don
Carlos, but he is bad to me and laughs at
me. I will throw it away. No, here !"
turning to him sharply, " keep it locked
up—I would n't have it, sir ! O, dear me !
I would n't look at it ! Tonita 's here—
well, Tonita is n't so bad to me as all you.
Here, Tonita," turning to her on her left,
" I 'll put it in my hair for you, because
you are quiet. Why, Tonita, you are
quiet. See here! what is it ? " She
leaned over in her chair and put one arm
on Tonita's shoulder and looked about
roguishly. " Wake up, Tonita ; it is
wedding-bells !" blushing again and smiling
at them all and never letting her little
tongue stop an instant. " Are you listening to them ? Is that it ? Come, now,
if that is it, you make me blush more by
being so still than by talking to me. Is it
that ? "

" Yes," said Tonita, smiling at her,
" that is it — wedding-bells."

Tonita still seemed sad, though she tried not to show it, and said jesting things to Ines, and fixed the leaf in her black hair. For a moment her eyes caught Ramon's. A little color flushed her forehead and she looked away again and busied herself with Ines. The latter was so much younger even than her years; an impetuous, stormy-hearted child, the uncontrollable life in her ebbing and flowing like the blood in her cheeks. In general, Ramon was plainly depressed. He would at times forget himself, then glance up quickly at Ines or at Don Carlos, rarely at Tonita, and join in the idle talk with but half-spirit.

" But Tonita's leaf, then," he said, " is higher than mine, Ines. Maybe I do n't like that ? "

" You ? Why, Ramon ! who said you ? " Ines put on a quizzical look of wonder and gazed at them all as though it were in the last degree absurd, her eyes dancing with ill-concealed delight. " Listen, all of you. Was there ever anything like this ? I said the leaf on my heart was for *some*body. This man here jumps at it that it is for him. Ha, ha ! Ramon !

You! You puzzle me, Ramon. Let me see — you are the fellow whom I never saw till you came one day to live here and tend Don Carlos's cattle. Why, I can scarcely recollect anything about you at all. It is so absurd, young man. Let me see — oh yes! You happened to go with me one day down by the stream. Ah, I remember. To be sure! It was you, was n't it?"

"What was it he said down by the stream?" said the Señora, delighted with the girl's mock artfulness. "Forgotten all that, have n't you? See her blush now, Ramon!"

The little irrepressible laugh that came up with the blush burst forth.

"O, *si, si!* — I have forgotten it all. Anyhow, it was not anything. I sang to him — there were some cattle down there. That was all. What did he say? O, how should I know what he said? Nothing, no doubt; except that the mesas were fine and the air seemed clear. O, dear me!" The light laugh, ringing and beautiful as a bird's note, dispelled the look of mock seriousness. Tonita's eyes were on her now — on the flush of the cheeks, the glisten of the hair. Tonita's eyes were sad and there was a deeper shadow in them.

"See here, little one," said Don Carlos, who had been watching her with a fond interest in his old eyes,—eyes a mixture of keenness, peace, and the natural pathos of age. "What will you do with yourself when you marry Ramon?"

"Do? Ah, why — O, well, ask Ramon!"

"You will just sit and think about me, won't you?" said Ramon.

"O, you boy! I can do that without sitting at all."

"No," continued the old Don; "how will you act, little one? What kind of a girl are you going to be, anyhow? Why, the idea of your being married! What will you do, little magpie?"

"Blush," said the Señora, "just blush the rest of her life away in a great, sweet blush,—that is it, is n't it, Ines?"

"I 'll tell you," said Carlota; "she 's going to do what everybody else does— she 's going to cook. Dear me, that is simple enough, Papa; cook, of course. It is Ramon who must eat it. That is not so simple, maybe. What do you say, Ines?"

"I know what she will do," said Tonita gently. "She is just going to be good."

"Well," said the Don, "little magpie, what do you say?"

Ines sat quiet, her eyes very wide open, thinking and looking across at Ramon.

"That is it," she said presently, sweeping the circle with her big eyes and speaking with a curt decision. "Tonita says it. Be good."

The old Don smiled, and tapped his fingers on the cloth as he leaned toward her.

"What does that mean, being good?"

Ines thought a moment more, with her eyes still very wide open.

"It means," she said slowly and weightily, like a justice delivering a verdict, "it means not to be like me!"

A general shout arose at this.

"O, ho!" cried Carlota, "what now? Going to be solemn, may be,— never laugh any?"

"Never blush any?" suggested the Señora.

"Why, that means — surely, Ines, that means," said Ramon, "not to love me!"

"No; I can wager my old eyes it is n't that," said the Don with a hearty laugh.

"What is it, Ines?" asked Tonita. "Does it mean that — not to love Ramon?"

"O," said Ines, annoyed, and mockingly pouting again, "no—it is n't that; not that I would n't love him. It just means—O, well, to be like Tonita!"

They all understood that. As they loved Tonita, so did they love this thing in Ines that made her adore Tonita. Tonita bit her lip slightly, and the flush came to her forehead again. She did not look up.

"Little magpie," said the old Don, leaning over to her and motioning emphasis with his forefinger at each word, "you are right. Just—you—keep—to—that!"

As soon as possible Tonita arose. She wandered a little listlessly through several

of the large rooms, and stood for a moment
before one of the fires, which crackled and
sent its sparks out at her. She did not like
the light, and wandered, still alone, out of
the door into the hollow square of the fort.
It was dusk, with a red flush in the sky
over the summits of the three mountains to
the left. The evening breeze came fresh
and slightly chill down along the western
plain that led to the peaks.

She stood a moment in the square and
looked at the ruined walls across, and at
the little old chapel, part of the wall at the
farther end. They would be married
there, she thought. She turned away and
walked round the end of the opposite wall,
and along the stream behind it, to the left,
away from the huts. On this side, too,
the willows and a few scrub-oaks stood in
groups upon the banks. Among these she
took her way. There was no path here,
but a sort of coarse sward covered the
earth down to the water's edge. She
walked on till she stood between the stream
and the lower corner of the fort. The
walls were all ruins here, and stood dark
and formless in the dusk, with great gaps

above and heaps of old adobes below, and arms of wall reaching out brokenly toward the water.

With her arm upon the limb of a little willow, and the angle of the ruined wall close behind her, Tonita stood and looked at the water flowing over the rocks, catching the last of the daylight in its ripples. There was a deep pain gripping at her heart. She stirred a little and caught the glint of the water far up the stream, and rested her head against her arm and looked blankly at the pebbles.

There was the snap of a twig down the bank of the stream toward the other end of the wall. It was followed by steps near her on the sward. Startled, she looked up and saw Ramon beside her. He was bareheaded, and by the light from the western sky she saw that he was pale. Immediately she moved as though to leave him, but rested her head against her arm again. For a moment he watched her.

"O Tonita!" he began, his voice shaking, "what is to be done?"

Tonita did not answer.

"I thought it would kill me,—all of her

talk and her laugh and her faith in me! God! I thought it would kill me!"

"Ramon!" cried Tonita, turning about and facing him. "Do not say anything more—for my sake, nothing more. Have we not said enough—all too much? There is but one thing to do. Heaven help us, Ramon, you know it as well as I. Why —why do you come near me?" The voice was very gentle, but broken almost to tears at the last.

"Because you alone, Tonita, can help me through it. Dios! but I am weak! I feel as though I could move mountains before I could do this—only when I am with you and you give me strength. I have it all from you; just as I love you, so have I the strength from you. I cannot do it alone!"

"Hush! Ramon, it is wrong that I speak to you—that I look at you. Oh! my heart! it is wrong that I must think of you day and night—day and night! But listen!" She drew herself up, and her white face showed a calmer firmness. "There is but the one thing. You must take her. Take her, and after a while, as soon as the excuse arises, you must go with her away. Ramon, I can bear it. You, too, you are strong enough to bear it. But Ines —Ramon, it would kill her. She knows nothing of herself, nothing of anything but that she loves you. It would kill her!"

There was silence a moment, Ramon with one hand upon the ruined wall, his white face set; Tonita leaning again upon the willow.

"I can bear it, Ramon," she said again. "Poor Ines—poor darling Ines! God pity her."

"God help a poor wretch like me!" broke in Ramon passionately. "Oh! why did n't I see it! Why was I so blind! It came so suddenly—even when I had hardly seen you, and she was always there and always singing and always happy. I tried—I tried, Tonita—God knows I tried that you should never know it, even that I should love her still; but I could not!"

"We both saw it at once," said Tonita. "No need of words, no need of silence. You could not have kept it back more than I. But, Ramon, it is the giving it up that will atone. Hear me, Ramon; look at me," she said, turning about and facing him again. "Let me show you how strong I am to give it up, that you may take strength also. Let me say it again as I stand here, let me break my heart saying it—that I love you—love you—love you with all the heart I have—say it only to show you that I can turn away, here as I do now, away from you, and leave you. And why? Because, much as my heart cries for you and breaks for you, it would not for the world, nor the heaven that I want in the world, tinge its own purity or break its own strength by taking you from her. God bless her — Ines, my blessed Ines! O Ramon!" turning her black eyes upon him again, "you will have the strength—you shall—my love shall be that strong. If it is the only way to give you power to do it, then my love shall be that strong. See now — I am willing!" She had stretched her arms out in abandonment to her purpose, and her slender figure was cut clear in the evening light against

the background of the mountains. The white face **was** whiter still, save for **the** flush of red about the temples.

Ramon turned away. He dared not look at her. He leaned his head upon his hands against the ruined wall.

"I will, Tonita," he said brokenly, "you know I will. There is nothing **else** to do, and it is for you—for **you**, Tonita; all I can give you now. You **have** been the only light in it all. I will not refuse you now. But it seems it will **kill me.** Every day I have seen the shadow of it— **every** smile she gave me, **every** blush, every laugh. I have done everything I could. I thought I loved her; I wanted to make her happy. Even **yet** I would not harm her for the world. But you—you, Tonita. I have seen you every minute of the day—the **very** breath of heaven came from you; and it seemed the ground under **my** feet **was** shifting, slipping away, leaving me only this to stand on—this sacrifice of yours and mine. And now—now **it is** only because it **is** yours and mine together that I can bear **it.** Heaven knows, I am **weak.** My love for you **is** too great.

Alone it would kill me. But it is that I am with you. Thank God, Tonita, that you are pure! Yes—I will do it. Perhaps I can bear it now. I will try."

Tonita bent her head upon the limb of the tree. The stream below her glistened like the eye of the dusk. She felt the mountain breeze blow her hair about her hot temples, and a great sob rose in her throat. Beneath the sweet gentleness of her nature there lay the native warmth of Spain, with all its power of emotion, making the sacrifice greater.

"Then go, Ramon," she said brokenly, not raising her head. "Go now. It is for her, Ramon, and—for me."

Ramon saw the hand she stretched behind her toward him, took it in his a moment, and turned and went away.

Tonita stood silent with her head upon her hand. She wanted to sink upon the ground and sob, but struggled with herself. Finally she raised her head and faced the breeze and let it blow over her face, and walked just a little and slowly up the stream in the dusk. The water beside her, and the plain stretching on up to the mountains, and the silent mountains themselves standing majestically against the sky, helped her in the struggle as nature had always helped her. She had known those mountains from her infancy, and they had never failed her yet. At last she turned, and retraced her steps about the wall, across the square, and into the house.

When she had gone, the figure of a man pushed itself through an aperture in the ruined wall, climbed over the pile of adobes that lay beneath, and came out on the bank of the stream. It was Juan. He had seen Ramon when the latter left the house, and, walking along the inside of the wall, had crouched in the ruins.

"So it is that," he said curtly to himself, his face showing malice. "Yes. So it is that. And the proud thing wants to throw herself away when it is as I said. So. The cursed Spaniard!"

He stood for a while and watched the water, grunting at times to himself. Suddenly he turned down the stream, along the wall, to the stepping-stones. He paused here and looked back for a moment at the old Don's house, where the light from the largest room shone through the window. He could hear his sister's laughter and the voice of Don Carlos. He turned away again and crossed the stream, followed the path, and entered the hut among the willows.

His mother had lit a candle which sat upon the table. She was washing some dishes, a cigarette still in her mouth.

" Well," she said sharply, " are you better in your mood? Are you still fixed in mind that your own blood is proud and that women are to live forever in two rooms and sit on dirt floors with no car- pets? Pah! you are ungrateful! A girl next to the best of them she is — and worth it. I wonder what have you been doing now ? "

Juan said nothing, but scowled at her. He sat down on the outside door-step and remained quiet for half an hour, looking toward the fort. He could still see the light from the window at the house of Don Carlos. It had grown quite dark when he saw Ines's form at last approach- ing the stream. There was some one with her, doubtless Ramon, and they stopped at the stepping-stones. Juan watched them silently. Presently Ramon left her, and she came up the path singing a wild little air to herself. She stopped in the door, with blushes on her cheeks and her hair hanging about her face. She looked like a child and was still gay.

"Ah!" she said, as she passed Juan and entered, "what a time it was! Mother, Don Carlos says he has half a mind to marry me himself! Good old Don Carlos!"

"And well he might say it — well he might!" cried the old Mexican, grinning.

Ines helped her mother with the dishes and told them what every one had said, and laughed and talked and sang the supper all over again, and danced a little between steps as she went to and fro. Juan sat still in the door and said nothing. His presence seemed to oppress Ines and finally she grew quiet. For a while yet she walked about doing various little things in the room, but saying nothing. Her vivacious spirits at last wore themselves out.

She took a second candle and lighted it

at the first and went into the rear room. Her mother lighted another cigarette and sat down in the door. Juan had arisen and gone inside. When his mother was fairly engrossed in her smoking, he went into Ines's room and closed the door.

His mother smoked one, two, three cigarettes. She heard them talking in the other room, but — pah! they were always quarreling! She was thinking about the golden future, with her daughter as good as the best of them, and herself living to have the rapture of it. Still she heard Juan's voice in the next room. That Juan was an ungrateful son! Would he never leave the child alone? But wait; Ramon would kiss out all that Juan could say, with one touch of his lips. Juan was always quarreling.

At last Juan came out and went away with a scowl upon his face, saying nothing as he passed her. He slept with some other vaqueros in a hut a little way down the stream. His mother arose and undressed herself and put out the candle. There was no sound in Ines's room. Ah! asleep, no doubt, thought her mother

— and dreaming of Ramon. Always
Ramon ! The old Mexican curled her
stiff limbs upon the bed and went to
sleep.

At ten o'clock there was still no sound
in Ines's room. The room was without light
as well, save for the faint light of the night
that came through the window. Ines had
not undressed herself. She lay without
moving on the bed, staring up dry-eyed at
the ceiling. Even had there been light to
see them, there were now no blushes on her
cheeks — only a pallor on the brown skin.
Nor was there any pout to the lips, which
were drawn tight. She was too stunned
as yet to think at all, save to wish in her
simple little heart that the Blessed Mary
would have her to die, here, now, before
she had more time to think. The darkness itself seemed the only relief to her.
She did not believe she could have borne
to see the things about her. The girl
that sang and laughed a little time before,
she thought must have been some other
girl. Already, at least, she must be a
good deal older. The half-stupor in
which she lay held but the two names float-

ing in it — Ramon and Tonita; sometimes their faces also. She could not banish these. Why could not the Blessed Mary permit her to die now? It would be simple enough, just lying here seeing their faces and trying not to think. That much she could bear.

At half-past ten she was thinking more coherently. She could not bear to lie still, and crept to the floor and stood a moment thinking it blankly. The wild little heart began to beat more violently now, and some of the old hot blood leaped to her face. A sort of pent-up sob broke on her lips, and she clenched her hands and leaned her weight upon the door. The blood was rushing in torrents to her forehead and her eyes, and she opened the door and caught the night breeze on her face. Turning again, she felt for the knife, where it still lay upon the table, and putting it in the belt of her dress, went out. She had no real intent to use it, but there was the wildness at her heart again that made her instinctively grasp the handle. No — as she went on haltingly in the night, she knew that she would not need the weapon. Tonita's face was too plainly before her, Tonita's heart too strongly weighing on her own, Tonita's life surrounding her, and breathing peace through the heat of her part-savage blood.

The moon had come up in the east, and stared blank and white over the mesas, and across the plains to the willows and the stream. She had little heed of her course, only that she might be away from them all. She walked slowly, with heavy steps, down along the stream, among the willows. The night air cooled her forehead, and laid bare the blank desolation of the fact. She did not wish Juan had not told her; she never thought of that. It was only that a great desert wind had come and carried it all away — everything she dreamed, or thought, or lived. It was as though there were nothing more anywhere upon the earth. She thought she might have seen the cloud of so big a thing coming. She knew not how to think, or what to feel, or where to turn. The great, empty night seemed to stand about a long way from her, cold and white, and just she alone lived in the middle of it, a throbbing heart with pain and desolation in its beating.

So, then, it was as she had feared. She wondered if that were it — her Indian blood. Oh! Blessed Mary! it was as she had feared! Her blood, her birth, the lack in her, the wildness that she could not tame. Why — they had not let her try — she could have softened it — surely she could have shown them it was no real part of her. The sense of helplessness that it was a thing lying back of her power to control — that it was no fault of hers, this alien blood, brought again the piteous sobs to her lips.

She went on blindly, following the stream. There were cattle down here, some standing about in the moonlight, some lying down—formless black shadows on the misty white of the plain. As far as she could see, away to the southeast, the broad valley stretched, dotted more indistinctly with the herds, growing more misty white in the distance, and fading into vague moonlight far away. Some of the cattle near-by turned their heads and faced her, and stood in passive wonder

The mistaken sense that she had been lacking in spite of herself, that it was the hated current in her veins that had changed it all, filled her with a vague feeling of guilt. Oh! why had they not seen it all before—why had they let her believe, and hope, and love so! What was the terrible God up there, where the sky shone white, that had branded this thing on her which she could not help? She wondered if the very stars could see that she was less than he; if the Blessed Mary hated the wild current in her veins; if, had she been given a little longer—just a little longer—she could have put it down, and kept his love. All she could conceive was that Juan had been right; that the brand on her had sickened Ramon's love; that the rapture of her short, impetuous life had burned itself out with the heat of her blood.

She had wandered perhaps a mile. A level space opened among the willows, with the stream sparkling through its center, and a few boulders strewn about. It was here they had come together that other day, when he had told her he loved her. She threw herself face down upon a rock, wishing she could sob her life out there. But the tears did not come; there was only the desolation and the helpless sense of lack in herself. For an hour she lay there, her heart aching. She went over every scene with him, recalled his every look. Twice there came over her a new, wild impulse. It was the spirit of revenge. She felt her hand grasp the hilt of the knife, while the blood seemed to leave her heart and rush in hot torrents over her little body.

But immediately Tonita's face came to her. No. That would be, above all else, what Tonita would have her put down. It was Tonita who led her— always Tonita. Then, too, that spirit of revenge, she thought, must be the hated blood in her. That was what she had tried so hard to put away. She would not turn to that now, go back to that part of herself that had caused it. Tonita would tell her, No, and she had said she would be like Tonita. A sort of wild pride came into her despair, a pride in putting down her impetuous self, now when he had turned away from it, and it made no difference. Not once did jealousy or hatred of Tonita enter her. She knew that Tonita had given him up to her. That was like Tonita—always so—always just as Ines wished that she herself could be. She could at least be true to Tonita in this, that she would not think of hating him, nor of revenge.

As the hour went by there was one other thing that came to her, grew on her minute by minute,—the temptation to end the despair. The untutored, savage element, turned from its natural course of hate, seemed to leap up and force her on to self-destruction. Her whole body tingled with the wild impulse—to cut away the despair that seemed to be killing her, to resent this thing that had been no fault of hers, to blot out the blank misery of the hour. The struggle grew terrible. She writhed in pain upon the rock. The savagery of ancient tribes seemed to bound in her veins. But there was Tonita still. She had conquered herself other times for the love of Tonita; would the

Blessed Mary only help her through this
—not let her lose Tonita's face a moment,
nor the eyes that had never turned upon
her with anything but love. This one
last thing—this hardest of all—she would
overcome for Tonita. Tonita had taught
her how; she would fight it out if it killed
her. That too, she knew, was the voice
of the blood she hated, the blood she
thought had turned him away.

Martyrs have suffered such as that; it
was the death struggle of the wild tribes
against the stronger nations from the other
world, brought down into one human heart,
and fought out there to the last drop of the
savage blood.

At last she arose and went back, still
slowly, but not hesitating. As she went
on, her brow grew cool, her heart calmer,
the purpose crystallizing in her mind.
Softly she crept to the hut where Juan
slept with the other vaqueros. She tapped
gently on the window, which she knew to
be beside his bed. Presently he was
aroused and had dressed himself and come
out, stupidly wondering at her.

" Get the horses," she said. " We will

go. Juan, I think you were right. I cannot stay. I will go with you."

Juan stared stupidly.

"We will go," she said again. "To Taos. Now."

Juan stood and stared and began to understand that he had succeeded. He was doubtful about this way of going in the night. Why not wait? She said what she could to influence him, almost in desperation lest she should fail. She dared not wait. Her tone finally persuaded him.

"But what of mother?" he asked.

"We must leave her. You can come again for her. Only—get me away!"

Two horses were silently procured, together with a sort of ancient carriage built with two wide seats and heavy wheels for mountain traveling. While Juan was about this Ines went to her room and lit the candle. She put on her hat and shawl, took a sheet of paper from a book Tonita had given her, and the pen and ink with which Tonita had taught her to write. When she had stilled her hand from trembling, she wrote a note and put Tonita's name upon it.

Over across the hollow square of the fort the old Don's dwelling lay in the quiet of the night. With swift steps Ines hastened to a door in the rear wall of the little placita, crossed the inner court with the moonlight falling on its bare, hard earth, and entered a hall that led to Tonita's room. The torrent of blood came to her face again and the blinding tears to her eyes. If she could only have dared to open softly the door and enter and see the face again! But she would not. She leaned against the door a moment and wet its panels with her tears and kissed the wood. Then she knelt and thrust the note beneath and turned and went back.

Juan was ready with the horses and had placed some few household things within the vehicle.

"Come," she said, "do not wait. You will come for mother again—when we are safe beyond the mountains."

She sunk upon the rear seat and buried her face upon the worn leather cushion, not daring to look back. Juan drove her away along the western trail, and the dis-

tant mists of the moonlight swallowed
them up.

In the morning, at the Don's house, they
were awakened by the voice of the old
Mexican raised in shrill lamentation in the
placita. They hastened out—the Señora
already filled with apprehension, Ramon
deep-eyed with loss of sleep—and found
her relating to Don Carlos, with excited
gesticulation, the discovery of her daughter's disappearance, and bewailing her own
forsaken condition.

In hastening to the placita Carlota must
pass through Tonita's room. She found
her sister standing, white and silent, with
the paper in her hand. Tonita sank upon
her knees beside the bed, moaning to herself:

" Oh! my Ines,—my poor darling Ines!"

Without lifting her face she gave the
note to Carlota, who took it and read. It
was thus, written in the girl's misspelled
Spanish :

" TONITA,—I go away because I want
to be like you in this too. Juan has told
me, and I want to give up Ramon for
you. I will try to be as you have taught

me how. I can bear it, Tonita, because you know it is the way you have taught me. There is only one thing that I cannot bear. That is, for you or him to come after me. Then I would kill myself. Do not do that if you want me to be good.

"Your Ines."

A COMPULSORY DUEL

THE stage-road ran along the foot of the mesa to a little "tavern" that stood among the rocks. The building, an erratic mixture of adobe and timbers, was a stranger to the art of architecture. There was little within several miles, except the house itself, the rocks, and the stage when it came. The bare prairie stretched far away to the front. Mr. Scaps, a smirking gentleman in a white apron, owned and operated the establishment, the operation consisting chiefly in serving bad liquor over a small and greasy bar in the front room.

Scaps had a daughter, who lived with him and took dilatory charge of the dining-room, when she could be induced to come out from Raton. She much preferred what she called "times" in Raton. She considered it dull out here at the tavern, but if it was dull when she was present, it must have been dead indeed when she was absent; for Maria had a way of turning things to her own account.

She was a small girl, and plump, with a habit of wrinkling up her forehead in resignation to some invisible unpleasantness. This habit of the forehead, instead of being objectionable, was deemed by Maria's acquaintances to have some peculiar charm of its own. It is certainly true that there was something about the girl's face (really not a pretty face, being too plump and too short) which had potency, and attracted men. In that boisterous and occasionally alarming style of love affair which characterized this unhampered territory, she was long since recognized as an adept.

She wore dresses that reached only to her shoe-tops, let her hair, neither very long nor of any particular color, hang down in a braid, and as a general rule carried her hat in her hand. In contrast to the expression of forehead already alluded to, it may be remarked that her mouth wore the perpetual promise of a laugh.

At the time that these things occurred, there were, besides occasional stragglers, three particular men who found much business at the tavern. When she had been in Raton, they were busy elsewhere ; two of them at least probably also at Raton. Now, that she had returned to the wilds of the stage-road, business with them had shifted. Milt and Smiley were cowboys and inseparable companions. They clung together through all variations of fortune, glued by the common interest of hope in Maria, like bees clinging to the same drop of honey ; each perhaps with some fear lest, should he loose his hold on the other, he might be deprived of the prey.

The third man had only happened in of late. He was a dapper little chap with some of the air of the town about him. He wore trousers wide at the bottom, and a cap thrown back anywhere among the irregular locks of his hair. One of these locks hung down over his eyes, which were shrewd and audacious. A cigarette was always in his mouth, usually hanging from his lips, helping thus to express a contempt for the world. This was Dix, of late formidable; for though the cowboys regarded him as absurdly young, they feared some unknown tactics, and mistrusted the air of the town.

"Got back earlier than usual to-day?" said the smirking Scaps, as Dix entered the bar-room about noon. Dix puffed at his cigarette and volunteered a conservative "Yes."

"Still havin' business up over the mesa?" inquired Scaps, leaning over the bar.

"Still seeing after the old gent's mining-stock over the range," said Dix, chewing his cigarette and waving the hair out of his eyes.

"The old gent, eh?" pursued Scaps.

"My dad."

"Minin'-stock, eh?"

"Yep."

"Where—where was it you said he lived?"

"Trinidad."

Scaps leaned back against the wall and eyed the younger man. His broad, flushed face expressed some disgust when Dix was not looking. Dix lit another cigarette, walked about pompously from one to the other of the two doors, perceived that they were both closed, and came and leaned over the bar. He put his chin in his hand and looked at Scaps with an air of complacent familiarity.

"She's a mighty fine gal!" he said presently.

Scaps winced a trifle, but smiled affably.

"She beats anything yet," volunteered Dix with assurance, after a moment's pause.

"Maria?" aimlessly queried Scaps.

"Scaps, I'll tell you what, she's— she's the very deuce of a girl."

Scaps began employing his hands with bottles and a corkscrew, looking all the while at Dix. The latter chewed his cigarette, took a full breath, and finally observed :

"I want her, Scaps."

Scaps suddenly stopped his movements with the bottles.

"Which?" he said with evident concern.

"Her, herself, Scaps. I want her."

Scaps dropped his jaw the fraction of an inch and stared, with the flush of his face deepening.

" Marry her, you know," said Dix.

The flush on the tavern-keeper's face still deepened. For a moment neither spoke, Dix's chin still resting on his hand and his face expressive of audacious assurance, Scaps standing staring at him. Presently the latter breathed heavily and set down the bottles ; then his wrath exploded.

" You sassy little idiot ! " he broke out. " Marry her, eh—marry her ? Well, not while Scaps is atop of the ground ! Why! you ain't got stuff enough in you to blow your brains out. Minin' stock, eh?— minin' stock ! I knowed you all along, and it 's a lie ! You seen her in Raton, and you come out here, and been workin' me blind. Minin' stock ! Look here, young man, you ain't got nothin' but what 's on your back, and your hoss. Now I 'll give you till to-morrow mornin' to clear out ; hear ? No little dried-up cuss with a cap on the back of his head ain't goin' to marry my gal. Till to-morrow mornin' ; hear ? "

Having said thus, Scaps shut up like a clam and turned stolidly about to the bottles and the corkscrew. Dix still leaned over the bar with his chin in his hand, eyeing the tavern-keeper. No whit of his assurance appeared to be abated. He puffed complacently at his cigarette and looked inscrutable. Finally he walked to the door, adjusted his cap farther back on his head, lit a third cigarette, and after a pause of complacent puffing quietly withdrew.

As Dix stepped to the rear of the tavern he beheld Maria some hundred yards or so up the side of the mesa, just disappearing behind a rock of unusual size. He who should think this coincidence one of unpremeditated chance could not be considered conversant with Maria's ways. Dix, too, climbed the mesa, stopping now and then on the way up to view the expanse of prairie scenery behind him and puff calmly at his cigarette. The plump Maria was sitting with her back against the rock when he casually sauntered round the corner of it. He stood in front of her with his feet apart and his cigarette hanging, and they looked at each other in silence.

" No go," said Dix at last.

" O, I knew it, I knew it! " said Maria with the wrinkle of resignation. " What 's to be done now, Dixie ?   Here I am— how are you goin' to get me ? "   She burst into a laugh.

" What 's the matter with the old cub ? " inquired Dix, removing his cigarette.

" Matter with him ?   Why, I 'm the matter with him ! "

" What makes him so deucedly particular ? "

" Milt."

" Milt ?   H'm.   Wants you to marry Milt ? "

" Wants me to marry his cattle and his three mesas," said Maria.   She arose friskily and danced about a little, whether in impatience or amusement Dix failed to perceive.   Then she leaned against the rock with her hat in her hand and laughed long and hilariously.   Dix eyed her with some wonder.

" Well—come to it, come to it," he said.

" O, Dixie, Dixie ! did you really think you could come it over the old man ?

You came out of it better than ever I thought.   Why," seriously, " he 's horrible !"   She did a little clog-dance over the stones with a very meditative expression of countenance. Dix stood by and puffed and looked on. She ended suddenly by pulling his cap down over his eyes and throwing his cigarette away.

" Wake up ! " she said sharply.

" What do you mean ? " said Dix.

" Well, ain't you goin' to do anything?"

" Why, thunder and lightning, what is there to do ? "

" You 've got to do something, you know, Dixie."

" Yes, according to the old cub, I 've got to clear out by to-morrow morning."

Maria wrinkled up her forehead and whistled.

" What ever got into him to give you so long!   He never did before ! "

" Call it long, eh ? "

Maria turned her back and burrowed her head against the rock.

" Plenty of time, Dixie."

" Time for what ? "

" Whatever you 're goin' to do."

" I did n't suppose you 'd do it."

" There ain't anything else."

" Run off, eh ? "

The girl turned about with the wrinkle on her forehead, and swung her hat by its cord round and round her finger.

" I 've thought it out many a time," she said. " I knew just how it would be. Looky over here." She went to the corner of the rock and pointed. The thumb of her other hand was in Dix's buttonhole, and Dix was lighting another cigarette and attending her remarks. " See the house down there. Me and you in it. Suppertime, you know. Then the sun 'll go down over this way. Look at that little ribbon of trail goin' away off yonder over the prairie—away off farther till it 's gone. That 's the way me and you 'll do. Tonight."

Dix looked out over the prairie, and puffed, and eyed the girl in calm admiration.

" Maria," he said meditatively, " you 're a bird. There 's just one thing. You never can keep Milt and Smiley off the scent. They 'll be back by three o'clock, and neither of 'em 'll take his eyes off you till bedtime. We can dodge Scaps."

The two stood in thought for some time.

" Maria," said Dix presently, " I am possessed of an idea."

" I knew it—I knew it!   What is it? "

" Can't you turn 'em against each other? "

" How? "

" O, you can turn 'em somehow. Tell Milt it 's Smiley, and Smiley it 's Milt, and lie about it, and—O, any way. You need n't tell me you can't do it."

" It 'd be hard—but maybe I could do it."

In the course of a half-hour, when Dix sauntered down the mesa, he was whistling gently to himself. A little later Maria descended from a different direction.

At eight o'clock in the evening two men quietly, even stealthily, mounted horses before the tavern and side by side, carefully eyeing one another, rode out over the prairie. They were Milt and Smiley, and, like Moses and the Children of Israel, they were seeking the back side of the desert.

Smiley was long and lean, and at present wrapped in despondency. His companion, always noted for melancholy, added to that general depression some little of suppressed wrath. Milt was a middle-aged man, whose peace of mind was easily wrecked. He sat nervously in his seat. Each man held a cocked revolver over the horn of his saddle; each kept his eyes fastened with deep suspicion on the face of the other.

The sandy trail led far out over the barren flats lying dim under the stars. The horses jogged with slow and regular beat of hoof. Perhaps two miles were traversed in absolute silence. The stars blinked on the motionless weapons, and the riders' eyes wandered not from their mutual gaze. It was Milt's deep, despondent voice that broke the silence.

" Might as well put up your gun. I ain't goin' to shoot till we git there."

" Put up yours first," replied Smiley, his gaunt face seeming to his companion to shine out of the darkness with dangerous hate.

" Stuck together a long time to be expectin' dirt-play now," said Milt.

" When I say ' three ' we 'll put up the guns, and neither one of us 'll take 'em out till we stand on the Cimarron bank ready fer business," said Smiley.

" Ready fer business," repeated Milt.

" One, two—you ain't goin' to fool me now, Milt?"

" Naw," in deep disgust; " go on."

" One, two, three."

The hammers of the revolvers were simultaneously lowered and the weapons stowed away. The silent march was continued, the horses walking very close together, the men still watching each other. Several miles more were traversed. There was no sign of human life for leagues about. Now and then the distant wail of a coyote came floating over the stretch of sandy soil. At last it was past nine o'clock. Milt's melancholy tones broke the silence once more.

" Why not right here—and git rid of it?"

" No, there's water there, and brush fer a fire."

" Fer a fire?"

" Might as well make a fire. More

light, you know.   Might as well do it
comfortable."

"How far is it?   I'm gettin' kind o'
sick."

"'Bout three mile yet."

Silence again, and the cushioned tread
of the horses.   Away in the east a very
faint tint of yellow suggested the moon
that would after a while appear.   A light
breeze played over Smiley's thin and rugged
features, flapped the brim of his sombrero,
and went over to Milt, and wantoned in
his tangled black hair.   The night was
terribly empty and depressing.   Milt was
feeling, or imagining, cold drops on his
forehead.   Even now neither man removed
his eyes for more than a few seconds from
the face of his companion.

They came to a huge bend in the course,
where the trail followed a curve of a little
stream.   It was nearly ten o'clock.   Both
men halted with their horses' heads over
the water.   They could hear the small
flood gurgling away aimlessly into the night.
Each man watched the other, and neither
moved.   Some minutes went by.

"You're goin' to do it fair, Smiley?"

"Why, pshaw! I 'm fair enough if you 're fair."

Neither dared to dismount before the other. The horses were growing restless and stretching their necks for the water.

"Count," said Milt.

"One, two, three."

The two men were on the ground at the same instant. Each keeping his steed between himself and the other, the animals were finally watered and picketed. The men stood again silently confronting each other.

"Who 's to build the fire ? " asked Smiley.

"If it 's all honest fair and nothin' 's to be done till we git the camp laid out, why, gad, Smiley, I 'll make the fire."

"I 'm fair if you are," said Smiley, suspiciously.

"Then here goes," retorted his companion. "You git the blankets."

"Blankets ? "

"Yes. I put two of 'em behind my saddle."

"What are they fer ? "

"Fer the feller that 's hurt."

There being still much suspicion and
much sidling, brush from along the stream
was finally accumulated, a bright fire made
to crackle and send its light up into the
darkness, and the roll of blankets brought
and placed upon the ground.   The blaze
lit up the trail before and behind for many
yards, and pushed the darkness like a wall
out into a great circle.   There was nothing to relieve the barren soil save the water
and the men and the blankets.   Turning
so as always to face Smiley, Milt unrolled
the blankets and spread them together by
the fire, Smiley meanwhile looking on
gloomily.

"Lot o' mess fer a dead man," said
Smiley.   His companion seemed to have
developed some old-womanish traits.   He
pottered about, still cautiously, however,
and stirred the fire and straightened the
blankets; the expression on his weather-
beaten, even wrinkled, face was one of
deepest dejection.

"Well," he said, "there's plenty o'
time and everything's to be fair, and we've
been good friends to one another.   Might
as well do everything right."

Finally the two men sat down on opposite sides of the fire, looking gauntly at each other. The revolvers were out again, each on the knee of its owner. Some ten minutes went by in silence. Milt's face grew older visibly, and there was an unwonted hardness about Smiley's lips.

"Smiley," said Milt.

"Well?"

"If it's me, Smiley—" He paused and looked mournfully into the fire; then proceeded:

"Smiley, if it's me, one o' the mesas is yours and the other two hers. The cattle goes even."

"It's uncommon good o' you, Milt."

"Well, I aint got nobody else."

Silence again for some time, each fingering his weapon.

"I aint got nothin' to leave," said Smiley. "If it's me, Milt—just so I'm put under decent, that's all."

"That's what the blankets is fer," replied Milt, looking across to the spot where they lay.

"We've hung together perty thick, aint we?" said Milt, after a time.

" And never had no trouble."

" We might 'a' seen it comin', though, Smiley."

" It was a mighty strong thing on both of us ;—O, it 's a natural enough end on it, considerin this here country."

" Natural enough."

The water rolled on into the night and the rim of the moon began to appear over the edge of the prairie, and still the two men sat.

" Do you mind the time you thought I stole your saddle, Smiley ? "

" I knowed right off it was n't you, Milt."

" Well, well—let it pass."

" There was one thing, Milt, I always had a mind to say, but somehow could n't come to it."

Milt waited.

" I done you dirt just oncet, Milt."

" When was that ? "

" It was a long time ago, and I 'd never do such a thing again. I ketched one o' your steers that was n't branded, and kept it."

" O, well—let it pass."

"Milt," after another pause, "I do think a heap o' that gal, honest."

"So do I."

Perhaps a quarter of an hour of silence, and Smiley's voice again.

"Might as well come to the business, might n't we?"

"I reckon so."

"It 's all fair now, Milt?"

"O, o' course—I know it 's fair."

Simultaneously the two men arose.

"We 'll go out here in the trail about twenty yards and stand off ten," said Smiley.

"Mind now, Smiley, here 's the blankets ready fer—fer whichever 's hurt, you know."

"Fer whichever 's hurt," repeated Smiley.

With weapons in hand and eyes fastened on each other, the men were on the point of starting. Suddenly there was the sound of horses' hoofs coming down the trail on a brisk trot from the direction of the tavern. The prospective duelists paused in nervousness. The hoofs came nearer, and out of the darkness grew two horses with riders. They came on into the brighter fire-light, and halted. The weapons dropped out of the duelists' hands. One of them was discharged, and the bullet plowed up the sand under the horses.

"Maria!" gasped Milt. Smiley's jaw was hanging. Maria leaned her plump body complacently against a great pack that was tied to the rear of her saddle. Dix, with the inevitable cigarette, and the cap for once on the front of his head, eyed the men in audacious amusement. He puffed a little, and said:

"Come on."

The horses started forward along the stream toward the rising moon, the cowboys stupidly staring after. A laugh rang into the night from one of the disappearing couple.

"Good-by, boys," came Maria's voice, wafted in gentle undulations on the breeze. "Do n't hurt each other—it 's naughty; and it would n't do any good." The laugh seemed to go away after her, and died with the sound of the hoofs.

For a moment, once again, the men looked at each other. Then they slowly sat down on opposite sides of the fire.

" She told me it was you," said Milt at last.

" Why, she told me it was you."

The realization of the fact stopped further comment for a time.

" She told me a lot o' lies about you, Milt."

" Me, too."

" It was her that done it about fightin'. She says I was n't worth her if there was n't no shootin' in it."

" She told me the same thing, Smiley."

" Why, I did n't want to shoot you, Milt."

" Well, it looked somehow like a cowpuncher ought to be up to anything o' the kind. That 's the only reason I done it."

About half-past eleven Milt arose. He looked dubiously at the blankets spread out smoothly upon the ground, then at Smiley, then again at the blankets.

" There they are, Smiley," he said dejectedly, pointing to them.

Smiley looked grimly into the fire.

" Which one of us is hurt, Smiley ? "

Smiley slowly arose.

" Come on," he said.

Together the two men lay down side by side upon the blankets, and wrapped their forms into one gray bundle.

The night grew deeper, the great moon came up into a barren sky and stared across the plain, and the fire went out.

At two o'clock in the morning Milt heaved a deep sigh.

" She was n't wuth it, anyhow, was she Smiley ? " he said.

" Naw," said Smiley.

THE DRIVER OF THE
OCATE

❧

I

A LITTLE adobe hut stood in the
valley between the mesas. A bay
horse was picketed three hundred
yards to the front. At the side, across
the trail that led away to the west into the
mountains, the little adobe stable held
several others. There was a well in front,
and a minute meathouse, adobe also, on
the other side, in what was for some
obscure reason called the garden. Some
two hundred yards to the rear a milch cow
was chewing her cud in a barren corral.
Beside the well were a wagon and a wood-
pile, and two dogs and a little boy played
about.

There was nothing else visible, except
the things nature had put there, for twenty
miles down the valley, across the brown
prairie to the east ; nor for three miles to

70

the west, between the mesas, till they closed the view and let the distant mountains peep over them; nor to the right or left, for a half or a quarter of a mile, to the mesas themselves, rising abrupt. If you had followed that New Mexican trail for eight miles toward the mountains, you would have come to another adobe dwelling, but it was too far away for moral effect.

The house comprised four little rooms, strung along one after the other, with doors between, too low for the Frenchman (who had built it himself, by the way) to go through without stooping. There was no front door—only two or three rear ones, which answered very well. Indeed, it would have been difficult to tell where the front of the house was, for, where it seemed to be, there was only an eye of a window, and no one ever went there, anyhow, for it faced no place where any one would want to go. The kitchen occupied about the middle of the house, with the lowest door of all opening out toward the well. The only room to the left of the kitchen was Mr. Frank's room, being the largest. To the right were two other rooms in succession, one of which was the dining-room. This last and Mr. Frank's room had doors also opening out toward the well and the wood-pile.

The boy, who had been picketing the bay horse, and had stopped to play with the dogs and mimic the coyotes, presently wandered into Mr. Frank's room. Mr. Frank lay in bed, with his white hair and beard, more silvery white and beautiful than seemed consistent with anything else in New Mexico, spread out about his face. His face was white also, but of a kind of whiteness that shone through a weather-beaten countenance. There was something almost pensive in his expression, or perhaps in the lack of it, and his eyes wandered about a little with a vacant stare.

Maggie, the Frenchman's wife, hovered about, arranging the old man's long night-gown, or straightening the covers. She was a born soubrette, having wandered somehow out of the East, and with the rugged solitude of this new Western earth only partially taming the soubrette spirit.

But there was unlimited kindness of heart in her eyes. She must have been thirty years of age, but she wore a short dress, coming just above the shoe-tops. It was easier to manage.

"Maggie," said the Frenchman, who sat far back in a big chair and smoked complacently, "he ain't gettin' no better. Tongue paralyzed."

"More than his tongue," said Maggie, touching her temple. "He does n't have any idea what we 're saying. His brain 's somehow wrong."

"Left hand, too, took a little. Seems stiff, kind o'."

The Frenchman's eyes opened and shut in immovable calmness as he puffed at his pipe. He was very tall and slender, with stooped shoulders. His weather-beaten face wore the expression of one whom long familiarity with the dangers of Western life had put beyond the power of being surprised. He was slow and good-humored, never conscious of a reason for excitement. His face was long, with a very large nose; his eyes and voice were almost gentle.

"How long since he come, Maggie?"

"Two weeks Sunday."

"Gettin' tired tendin' to him?"

"O, I do n't mind—gives me something to think about." She hummed a little flippant tune and went to the door. "He is n't a great deal of bother, only he will get up when I 'm not watching, and he goes tottering around, mumbling."

Something seemed to attract the paralytic's attention. He raised his head a little from the pillow. One thin hand was stretched out on the bed. He mumbled incoherently to himself:

"Whuzz'a—whuzz'a—whuzz'a—."

The sound seemed like some broken question beginning, "What 's the—." It stopped with the second syllable, however, and after several repetitions trailed off into mumbling. The old man stared vacantly at the door.

"Whuzz'a — whuzz'a — whuzz'a—," he said again, after a moment.

The dogs suddenly set up a furious barking without, and two horsemen rode to the door.

The old Frenchman stiffly arose, still puffing, and went out.

"Why, it's the Giant," he said, "and Lebi."

"It's us," said the Giant, a man of huge frame and massive jaw, riding a black horse. Behind him, on a smaller animal, rode a little, swarthy Mexican with great lips and glittering black eyes.

The Frenchman puffed silently at his pipe, eyeing the new-comers. After a moment he said:

"Get down?"

"Got room fer us?" inquired the Giant.

"Oh, such as there is."

The two dismounted.

"Picket your horses out there any place," said John, as he stooped through the kitchen door, and entered the house. Maggie, accustomed to such demands on her hospitality, began preparing supper for six instead of four.

"Who are they, John?"

"O," said John, evasively, "they're fellows from Wagon Mountain. I used to know 'em up in the mountains. Reckon I know everybody, eh?" he continued, with a broad smile.

" Whuzz'a — whuzz'a — whuzz'a —" came from the old man in the next room.

" Never you mind, Mr. Frank," called Maggie, cheerily. " It 's only visitors. I 'll have your supper ready pretty soon. My!" to John, " he 's always hungry— and eat—whew!" she whistled a little on a high note.

The two travelers came in, the Mexican stopping by the door and the Giant being in a formless way introduced to Maggie. After some fifteen or twenty minutes they sat down to a supper of oatmeal and pancakes in the dining-room. Maggie was occupied during most of the meal, however, in feeding Mr. Frank in the rear room.

The Mexican said absolutely nothing, but ate voraciously, with his head low down and his black eyes on his plate. The Giant, too, was unusually quiet. It was some time before he said :

" Who 's him in there?" pointing toward Mr. Frank's room with his thumb.

" That's old Frank," said John.

" Which, the driver ? "

" Same."

" Him that drove the Ocate stage ? "

" Same Frank."

" What's wrong ? "

" Got laid up, somehow. You know he quit the Ocate last March and went over on the other trail. Had n't heard nothin' from him till I went over to Watrous and found him laid up, with some Mexicans half tendin' to him. I brought him here."

" Fever? "

" Paralyzed a little, looks like. Wrong in his head — can't talk."

" How 'd it happen? "

" Could n't find out. They said he come wanderin' there in the night. He 's never been in his head since. O," with a gentle calmness, " he's gettin' old, you know, gettin' old—like me."

" Whuzz'a — whuzz'a — whuzz'a—," came from the other room.

" O, you 're spilling it, Mr. Frank, you 're spilling it! " they could hear Maggie say.

"H'm!" said the Giant, in meditative surprise; "so that's him that drove the Ocate fer eight years, an' was the sharpest-eyed man in the territory."

"You ought to knowed," said John, with his mouth and huge nose joining in a smile, to himself.

The Mexican gulped audibly, and ate faster, saying nothing.

"Well, that he was — an' pluck — Lord!" said the Giant. "Yes, I ought to knowed."

No one spoke for a while.

"That old man's seen wild times, ain't he, John?"

"He's been through a heap—who ain't, out here? You know he had a little ranch some twenty years ago down by Tiptonville. Wife died, and he went out prospectin'. Went clean to Alaska oncet. Come back and went on the trail. Never had but one son, I guess, and he run off. Old man's clean alone—just Maggie and me. Maggie's mighty good."

An hour later the night had come, and an early moon was shining. Mr. Frank was asleep, and Maggie and the boy were in the front room. As the Frenchman leisurely returned from some last attention to the horses, walking a little bent, and still smoking, the Giant stopped him at the wood-pile.

"Thought I might as well tell you what we 're after, John."

The Frenchman stopped, and puffed, with one hand at his pipe, scrutinizing the Giant.

"'Cause you 've always been neutral, an' in no ways notionate about us fellers, an' you 'd better know what we 're goin' to do."

"You ain't goin' to hold up the stage a bright night like this?"

"No, it ain't that."

"Well?"

"You know me an' Lebi quit the gang a month ago, an' been stayin' at Vegas an' one place an' another, like white people, teamin' an' cow-punchin'."

"And I was mighty glad of it—it was time—by the Lord, it was time!"

The Giant shifted a little uneasily from one foot to the other, and the Frenchman waited.

" But you know Pete an' Laskins still held the old game."

" Nothin' 'll stop Laskins. But Pete —he 's young to be in the business."

" He 's an ungodly good hand at it."

" Well ? "

" Well, there 's a price on them two fellers' heads."

" So I heard."

" A thousand apiece."

" So I heard. What 's it for ? "

" Some piece o' work over on the Baldy trail. The sheriff at Wagon Mountain 's got the money to hand to the man that brings 'em in, dead er alive."

The two men looked at each other in silence for a moment. The Mexican had come out, and was crouched in a heap by the well, several rods away.

" Well ? " said John.

" We 're goin' to do it, John."

The Frenchman puffed, puffed, with no move or expression.

" They 're in the same old place—up around Garrett Peak. We know it like a book, Lebi and me."

Still the Frenchman made no reply, but silently puffed at his pipe.

"I hate the Mexican, but he 'd sell his soul for a thousand dollars."

John leaned against the wood-pile, and looked down the long meadow, where the Wagon Mountain trail showed itself faintly in the moonlight.

"It 's got to be done delicate," said the Giant.

The Frenchman made no reply.

"I can signal 'em easy, an' we 'll drop in on 'em an' make it up again to go back to the business. They 'll take it straight, an' like enough fix up a job right off— with four of us."

The Mexican shifted a little, drawing his knees up close to his face, making a black bunch out of himself.

"We can wait till they 're asleep, then you know—jus' one apiece. Both these horses can carry double."

There was silence for a long while, with the Frenchman meditatively smoking.

"It 's a rotten piece of business," he said slowly, at last.

"It's accordin' to the law," said the Giant.

"A rotten piece of business," repeated the Frenchman.

"Well, Lord, yes,—I ain't hankerin' deep after the pleasure in it, not by a devil of a sight—Lord!"

The Frenchman thought a moment more.

"I'd kick tremendous hard on it if it was n't for Laskins. That man ought to be hung—hung nine times, if he'd stand it. I'd like to see him get it any way there is to give it to him. He's the most hellish desperate man in the mountains, and dirty mean. But Pete."

The other made no answer.

"Still, he's done enough to deserve it," said the Frenchman. "He's a bad man —pshaw! we're all bad enough. But somehow I always liked Pete."

The Giant did not reply.

"You're a cussed set of fellows," said the Frenchman after a pause. "You're a cussed set of fellows. If it was n't for riddin' the country of Laskins——. It'll be a dirty trick."

" It 's the only way to do it. Long-eyed Pete an' that devil of an Englishman ain't caught no other way."

" When are you goin' ? " asked John.

" Start up to-morrow mornin'. Get there in the night some time."

The two stood thinking for perhaps three minutes. Then the Frenchman started in, smoking still.

" Recollect," he said pausing, " this is your business and none of mine. I don't believe I in no ways approve. But I 'm neutral, like you said, and you fellows can fight it out amongst you. You 'll be comin' back this way ? "

" Yes, that 's why I told you—we 'll have to come back this way."

" Well, it 's your own business. Stay here to-night, o' course, but I ain't in no ways approvin' of the thing. It 's a dirty piece of business."

He re-entered the house.

" Maggie," he said, " put some beddin' on the kitchen floor for 'em. They 've got a long ways to go and had n't better start till morning."

The Giant meanwhile stood by the

wood-pile for several minutes, looking down the meadow.

"Come on," he said at last to the Mexican. The latter arose and silently followed him into the house.

At nine o'clock in the morning, with a bright sun over the mesas, the two brought their horses to the well and prepared to start. The boy and the Frenchman and his wife came out to watch their departure.

"It's a long piece you've got to go, is it?" asked Maggie.

"Lord, yes," replied the Giant; "way up past Cimarron."

"You won't get there before night?"

"No, hardly before mornin'."

"Live up that way?" asked Maggie, looking up with her sharp eyes.

"Well—, O yes—yes, you might say so. We used to live up that way."

"Well, good luck to you," she said, starting in the house whistling a little tune.

"We'll be back this way before long, I reckon."

"O," she said, stopping in the door and eyeing them again with her head on one side. "You'll be back?"

There was a fumbling at the door of Mr. Frank's room. The door opened, and the old man, dressed in his nightgown, came tottering out before Maggie could stop him. He seemed dazed, and stared at the horses and groped about.

"Whuzz'a—whuzz'a—whuzz'a—"

"Oh! Mr. Frank! Mr. Frank! come back inside—mercy me! You'll catch your death of cold!"

She took him by the hand as she might have taken a child, and led his wandering steps back into the house. The men could hear him still mumbling.

"That's him," said the Giant, rather to himself than to any one else. "Lord! I'd know him anywheres. Pore old man!"

With that the two rode slowly away toward the west.

"John," said Maggie, as they watched the riders through a rear window in Mr. Frank's room, "I do n't like those men."

John made no reply.

"John?"

"Well, Maggie?"

"Those men are n't very good sort of men; you know it."

"O—we ain't none of us good out here, Maggie."

"But they're bad, are n't they, John?"

"Lord, Maggie, it's owin' to what *is* bad. I reckon we're all bad. A man *has* to be bad."

"No, but John—are n't they real, unusually—very, very bad?"

John puffed a little.

"No, Maggie; unusually bad?—no, I do n't know as they are."

II

The early moon again, and the eastern sky white with it as it rose higher toward the zenith. The mesas had been left behind and the trail was climbing ruggeder heights. All about stood giant rocks and craggy precipices, some higher, some lower, some abrupt against the sky, others yonder in the distance. The moonlight robbed the scene of form and added to it beauty. Breezes in pine trees made a lonesome sort of music; otherwise the silence seemed a positive thing of potency. The horses clambered over the stony way, and stopped and puffed, and clambered over the way again, and got on somehow —anyhow—through the night. The Giant rode in front, leading the way, and Lebi followed, kicking his horses' sides regularly with its steps after the resultless manner of the Mexican.

"Then what did you come for?" said the Giant, breaking a long silence which followed the sound of the Mexican's complaining voice. "You cussed Mexicans are cowards, every one o' you."

Lebi rode on in silence for a while, the reins hanging on his horse's neck, his own head drooped in sulky meditation.

"Me no coward," he said presently. "Me rob stage all 'lone when you 'n' Laskins dead drunk at Ocate."

"With one man in it, an' him a consumptive—a devil of a fine piece o' work! An' you carried off my end o' the swag, I'll bet you that."

"You liar!"

The Giant suppressed a laugh of contempt that nevertheless got out into the night and echoed a little among the rocks. He would have laughed so at a coyote that followed his horse, or a snake that rattled at him as he passed.

"Liar, eh?— well, let it go at that. You got more than your share by the agreement, anyhow ; an' I did n't believe then, an' I do n't believe now, that that stage carried only two hundred dollars. But, Lord, you can have it."

"Me no got it, me no had it, me no want your money. You liar."

"I wonder who 's the liar. Cowards are generally liars."

"It 's the sneakin' lika this, where it 's devilish shut in up yonder, what me no like. Long-eyed Pete no easy man—no catch him 'sleep."

"Did n't I tell you he knows my whistle? Now stop your baby-talk. No —O, no! — you 're no coward. You robbed the stage by yourself the other side of Ocate when me an' Laskins was drunk. If you was so brave then, what's the matter with you now ? I 'll bet you done it because you was too big a coward to keep from it, with us on the other side o' the ridge to cuss you if you did n't. I 'll bet them bow-legs o' yours shook like a knocked steer's. Maybe Pete an' Laskins are gettin' ready to rob the same stage when she goes through to-morrow night. Stir yourself up an' show us some o' your Indian blood. O, no, you 're no coward. Do you know who it was drivin' the stage the night you robbed the consumptive ? "

" No," moodily.

" It was that paralyzed old man back yonder."

" Dios—no! "

" Well, that 's who it was—him with his white hair an' his totterin' an' his nightgown."

The Giant stopped his horse for a minute's breathing where a little elevation lifted his form against the moonlit sky. He turned with one hand on the beast's hip and eyed the Mexican, who stopped just below him.

" Him that that woman's puttin' to bed like a baby."

" Him no baby then," as though sheepishly defending himself.

" Well, I reckon not, considerin' the welt you carried off on the back o' your head. If he was n't such a corpse an' paralyzed, he 'd 'a' recognized you to-day an' gone off clean crazy."

" Him no would know me."

" There 's where you 're wrong," and the Giant spurred his horse on again, and the march was resumed. " He run that stage fer eight years, an' he knowed every dog's son of us like books."

" Him no sabe 'bout me."

The Giant laughed softly to himself.

" That's the reason we was drunk at Ocate. He knowed us an' you was new to these hills then."

" You 's cowards—you 's cowards ! "

" That's discretion, you chicken; that ain't cowardice. He knowed us an' he did n't know you. But he 'd a' knowed you again after settin' eyes on you once ; no matter about your mask an' the dark. He was the sharpest-eyed gent anywheres on the road south o' Denver then.

The Mexican rode on in silence for a moment, eyeing the Giant.

" You wanted him kill me," he said presently.

" O, no, we did n't. We wanted you to come out jus' like you did, but we did n't have no idea you would. If you had n't been such a coward you 'd 'a' dropped in it. You did n't think anybody seen you, did you? I was drunk at Ocate, was I? What for did you sneak out after the stage was past an' sneak up an' club the consumptive onto the floor an' git the drop on the driver from behind, eh?"

The Mexican said nothing, but followed along like a cursed cur.

"You could n't 'a' held him up in front, could you? Devil a bit, fer you 're a Mexican, the rottenest set o' people on God's earth—worse 'n niggers, I 'll be cussed."

"What you leave it fer me all 'lone, then? You 's cowards!"

"Because you was new in the gang an' we wanted to see your spunk. The rest of 'em was satisfied with it—but I seen the act an' I knowed then you was a coward, an' I 've knowed it ever since."

"Pete shy off. Him no would go that night. Him coward."

"There ain't a drop o' coward blood in Pete an' you know it, if he does git the sulks."

" Pete say nothin' an' sneak off dam 'fraid."

The Giant laughed scornfully to himself.

" Afraid o' nothin'. Pete 'd hold up the devil—an' do it in front too. As fer sayin' anything, he never did say anything. Pete 's the silentest man in the business. An' he always shied off from that Ocate stage-road. I never could git him to tackle it. He 'd walk to the Vegas road an' hold up the Baldy mail afoot before he 'd go a dozen steps fer the Ocate stage. Somehow he hated that road. Afraid, eh? Never had none o' that in him—you had it all. It was him that first shied off an' left the job fer you an' argued fer the tryin' o' your spunk, but there 's no afraid in long-eyed Pete."

There was silence for a quarter of an hour, the Giant meditating and the Mexican following along like the cur still, while the white moonlight dimly revealed new ravines to cross and rugged ways to climb.

" Yes, you 'd 'a' swallered bullets that job, if you had n't sneaked up behind," mused the Giant again, after a while. " Fer that old man's eyes was like buzzard's eyes, an' he was as quick as forked lightnin', by the Eternal—him that 's there now—same old man—with his whiskers white like that moonshine, an' his eyes wanderin'," continuing dreamily to himself, "—wanderin'—an' that graveyard voice o' his, an' his nightgown, an' John's wife tendin' to him like a baby—jus' like a little baby."

Two hours' farther ride, for the most part in silence, and it was near midnight. The moon, near the zenith, still shone brightly. The trail now wound about the base of a huge cliff and suddenly started up, through a broken gorge, toward the top of a bald peak. It became less of a road, very narrow and rugged, precipitous, and flanked by shrubs and rocks.

The horses breathed more heavily as the ascent grew steeper and the atmosphere rarer. There were cliffs on either side now, a sort of narrow, gigantic aisle with a still cataract of rocks down between, making, or marring, the path. Now and then the Giant, as he rose higher and higher above the regions they had traversed, turned his head and looked back through the aisle between the cliffs into the distance, where scores of miles of mesas and prairie lay jumbled together in moonlight. The Mexican looked stupidly at his horse's head.

An hour of this and they approached the top. Just where the cliffs began to relent and join the summit of the cataract of rocks and flow into each other, the Giant stopped and whistled. The signal echoed faintly behind, and in front a light breeze carried it on among the pines of the summit—three short notes with a longer one an octave lower. A sound, as of some one suddenly breaking twigs by starting, came faintly from above, several hundred feet away. The Giant listened a moment and repeated the whistle. He got for answer a weird cry like the cry of a " piñonero," repeated three times.

" That 's Pete," said he.

The horses were spurred on again and entered a little mountain park, like a rolling lawn, a hundred yards square, and almost surrounded by rocky elevations. Pine trees here and there converted the lawn into a grove. The earth was covered with a soft sward, and rocks on all sides gave the place an air of snugness. The moonlight revealed two horses picketed at the farther end, their heads now suddenly erect, staring at the intruders. The almost dead embers of a fire blinked a little in the shadows of some shrubs.

"Who's there?" cried a deep voice from near the fire, and a form arose, obscuring the light.

"Lebi, of course—an' me," said the Giant, as the two rode forward.

"O — I knew it was you," replied Laskins, to whom the deep voice belonged. "What in the devil's name are you doing here?"

The Giant laughed a little to himself.

"You do n't suppose I 've forgot my trade, do you?" he said.

"No; but you 've turned too devilish white for this kind of thing, both of you."

"Do n't be too sure o' that. Cuss white livin', anyhow. It 's damn tiresome."

Laskins eyed him with a suspicion not visible in the dim light. The Mexican, behind, said nothing, but followed the

Giant's example in picketing his horse. The two returned to the fire and threw their great saddles upon the ground.

"Where's Pete?" said the Giant, as he looked about him. The Mexican meanwhile crouched silently by the fire and warmed his hands.

Laskins said nothing, but moved toward the embers, where his blanket lay.

"Where's Pete?" repeated the Giant.

"He's over there on that rock," said Laskins, pointing carelessly with his thumb.

"Pete!" called the Giant.

No answer.

"Pete!"

"Well." The word came, accented with a little impatience, from the rock.

The Giant walked to the spot.

"What in the name o' holy mass is the matter with Pete?" he said half aloud.

Where the moonlight fell full on a huge, square rock, was revealed, half lying upon its summit, his chest down and one hand supporting his head, the figure of a man. He appeared not tall, lithe, almost slender, but powerful. His face was in the shadow of his sombrero. He lay still, looking down along the side of the rock.

" What 's the matter, Pete ? "

" Nothing," without moving.

" Sick ? "

" No."

" Got the dumps, eh ? You 're the moodiest man in the business. Anything wrong ? "

" No, no—of course not." He still lay in the same position, not even turning his head toward the questioner.

" You knowed it was me, did you ? " said the Giant. " Have n't forgot the old whistle ? "

" You heard me answer, did n't you ? "

The Giant stood looking at him a moment, and turning, went back to the fire, which the Mexican had by this time stirred into a small blaze. Laskins was sitting beside it also.

" What 's the matter with Pete now ? " queried the Giant, taking his seat beside the others.

" O, Lord knows," said Laskins with a sort of uneasy impatience. " What always was the matter with him ? "

" Aint he got over that yet ? "

" He gets worse. What in the devil are you fellows here for ? " still with suspicion in his eyes.

" We 're here, old man," said the Giant, " to go back to business—that 's exactly what we 're here for. Damn bein' civilized ! They 're against us, every man's son—there 's nothin' in it. I 'm dead sick o' bein' a Sunday school man, anyhow. I 'm ready fer business, right now—how about you, Lebi ? "

" Me all ready—dam Sun' school man!" said the Mexican, moodily.

Laskins looked quickly from one to the other and back again. His eyes were sharp and small for one of his huge frame, and long custom had put them forever on the alert. Apparently he was not quite satisfied.

" Where you been all this time ? "

" Santa Fé — Vegas — Lord knows where. Denver once. Been punchin' cows an' drivin' teams an' a lot o' rot business."

" What made you quit ? "

" Could n't stand it—Lord !" with a

shake of his great head, " could n't stand it ! It's too slow, Laskins," lowering his voice to a confidential tone ; " I 'll tell you what, old man, that kind o' business is too ungodly slow."

Laskins continued to ply him with questions and finally breathed more freely. The thing seemed clear enough. He never had understood how the Giant could be satisfied with the ways of civilization ; he had always thought he would come back. Laskins becoming more at ease, the conversation grew freer. Furthermore, he had good reason to rejoice at the return of the wanderers.

" I do n't know what in the world to do with that fellow," he said presently, lowering his voice and pointing to the rock where Pete still lay.

" What's up ? " asked the Giant.

" There was a tall sight up — but he 's knocked it in the head."

" Won't he go ? "

" You could n't lasso him and haul him. He 's been that same way for three weeks. I had the prettiest job you ever saw fixed up for to-morrow night. There 's to be a thousand dollars in gold in the Ocate stage, and I can't get him to budge."

"Lord, he never would go after the Ocate stage — did n't you know that?"

"But it 's everything else alike. Last week we had it laid out to touch the Taos mail — no go. He would n't stir. Half the time he hangs around on that rock, or under a tree somewhere. Oh — curse such unsteady hands, anyhow! I 'm sick and tired of him."

"He 's the best man the gang ever had when his head 's straight," said the Giant.

"That 's the trouble of it; the spoiling of a work of art, that 's it — the spoiling, by thunder, of a work of art."

"Well, let him sulk. We three can handle the stage to-morrow night."

Laskins's eyes lit up with exultation. He chuckled to himself.

"Ready right off, eh? It 's a go."

"It 's a go, old man," said the Giant, nodding his head slowly and eyeing Laskins. "You 're right, it 's a go — eh, Lebi?"

"Me no coward," said the Mexican.

The matter settled, Laskins rolled up

in his blanket and in five minutes was snoring comfortably. The Mexican crouched close by the fire, warming his hands, saying nothing. For a few minutes the Giant sat still, staring at the red embers in a half dreamy way, and listening to the regular evidence of Laskins's slumber. Finally he arose and, leaving the Mexican by the fire, walked slowly through the moonlight to the place where Pete's form still lay black against the gray rock. The latter's position was unchanged. He lay with chest down and head raised on one hand, looking at the ground below.

" Asleep, Pete ? "

" No."

" Not sick, Pete ? "

" No."

" We 're goin' after the Ocate stage to-morrow night — Lebi an' me have come back to the business. Goin' with us ? "

" No."

" It 's a devil of a fine job — a thousand dollars in gold. Not many passengers this time o' year. Better go. It 's like findin' it."

" Think I 'm afraid, eh ? "

" Not you — not hardly," with a confidential laugh. " You afraid ? Not scarcely, Pete."

Silence for a moment.

" Look here, Pete."

Still silence.

" What on earth 's the matter with you, anyhow ? "

No answer.

" Sick o' the business, eh ? "

Still no answer.

" Pete, I wish to the devil you 'd tell a feller what 's wrong. Lord, ain't we all hung by you before this ? "

" You 've been all right," said Pete.

" Ain't we all been like a family, Pete — ain't we ? "

No answer.

" Ain't we been proud o' you, Pete, an' made a heap o' you, an' ain't the thing paid ? "

Pete moved a little uneasily.

" It ain't your conscience, is it, Pete ? "

The silent man rested his head on his closed fist.

" Conscience, eh, Pete ? " ·

Still no answer ; Pete still looking along the edge of the rock to the ground below, the moon casting the shadow of a waving pine twig, like a finger, across his face.

"H'm —" said the Giant, "sick o' the business !"

With his feet apart and his hands in his pockets he stood silently watching Pete. Neither moved. One, two, three minutes went by. Four minutes, and Pete sighed a little to himself. Then he turned his face toward the Giant, raised his head from his fist, rested his hand on the rock, slowly rose to a sitting posture, still leaning on his hand.

"Yes, by God !" he cried suddenly, his voice suppressed so that it sounded deep. "Sick o' the business — sick o' the whole hellish business ! Look here — you 've known me a long while — you know I 'm no chicken-hearted coward. You 've been kind o' good to me all this time, for I was younger than you fellows. I might as well tell you." His voice became more excited, though even lower, and his eyes shone. There was an odd expression about the mouth.

"Three weeks ago we robbed the Baldy mail. You never—you never—heard me say anything about my havin'—a father hereabouts, did you? He used to drive the Ocate. Lord God, I wish he was there yet!" He rubbed his forehead with his free hand for a moment in silence.

"You know the Baldy road—it was there where the trail turns off to Romero's place. I can see it now, I can. Lord God! I can see it now! There was n't no light much, and I was to take her in front and Laskins was behind. She pulled down the trail with one of her lights out, and I could n't see plain. The rocks come up there high on both sides—you know. We were behind 'em, and when she got opposite we jumped out and stopped her. I could n't see what Laskins was doin'— Lord knows I could n't see nothin' well. The driver come at me over the horses' hips with the butt of a Winchester—the thing surely was n't loaded. The off horse began plungin', and there were two men inside screamin'. I saw the driver raise up again, and somehow I did n't want to shoot. There was n't a minute to stop, and I jumped onto the doubletrees and came up at him, grabbin' his wrist with my left hand, and gave him a blow with the butt o' my gun on the side of his head. God! I can hear him groan yet, and he kind o' crushed all up together, and rolled off limp as a rag right on top o' me, knockin' me down. I knew it then—I can't tell how, but I knew it then. Something in the feel of him, maybe, while I was crawlin' out from under him, or his hair rubbin' on my face, or maybe the way he groaned—Lord God knows what, but I knew him.

"I could n't think o' nothin' else. I got up and he lay there in the road. I felt dazed, kind o', and I went and got the light. I guess Laskins had fixed the passengers, and was gettin' the mails. I came back kind o' shaky in my knees, and came near fallin' on him again. I took and turned his head around so as his face was up. Somehow I could n't bear to turn the lantern on it—O God! God! After a while standin' there, not darin' to look, got worse 'n lookin', and I shut my eyes first and turned the lantern round, and got down on my knees beside him. Then I looked,

and the blood was runnin' down his cheek
and his eyes were starin', half-open. It
was him. I did n't know no more till I
came to in the scrub-oak, up on the mesa,
where Laskins dragged me. Laskins had
the money, and the stage was gone, and
the passengers had took the old man off—
Lord knows where—Lord knows where!"

His voice had grown almost monotonous.
He sat quite still when he had finished,
leaning on his hand, looking out across the
grove. Presently he shuddered.

"I can see him now—I can see him
now!" His hand wandered through the
air as though tracing out the scene; his
fingers looked long and powerful and, due
to the moonlight, white. "O my God!
I can see him now!"

He sank back on the rock and rested
his forehead on both hands.

The Giant watched him in silence, his
hands still in his pockets, his feet still
apart. Presently he spoke :

"Pete."

There was no answer.

"You do n't reckon you killed him, do
you Pete?"

A shudder shook the form on the rock, but there was no sound.

"No, now Pete, you don't want to think that."

The Giant shifted his weight a little to the right foot, and hung a thumb nervously in his vest pocket. After a moment more of silence he spoke again:

"'Cause you see it ain't likely.'

Pete kept his head on his hands and said nothing. The Giant shifted to the other foot, and worked his fingers nervously.

"It 'd take a mighty oncommon lick like that, you know, Pete."

Stillness again for a little while with the finger of shadow across Pete's face.

"You know it might 'a' jus' stunned him, Pete. It might 'a'—" The Giant paused hesitating. He was still more uneasy in manner. Several minutes went by with no change in either.

"'Cause a man like him 's tough, Pete —it ain't no ways likely."

No move from the figure on the rock, and another pause.

"It might 'a' jus' kind o' laid him up a

little, you know. Pshaw! 'taint no ways
likely, Pete, sure now."

The Giant began to feel an unusual
perspiration on his forehead.

" Why, you know that feller at Wagon
Mountain—Lord, you know we all beat
him up like that, an' it jus' made him sick
a little."

Pete twisted somewhat and clenched one
of his hands slightly under his head.

" 'Cause an' old man what 's been drivin'
stages that long 's tough, Pete—mighty
tough."

But it seemed Pete was beyond answering.

" He 's bein' took care of somewheres
—you can 'low on that."

The Giant somehow found it equally
hard to go on and to stop. After another
pause :

" Some woman now, likely. They must
'a' all knowed him—Lord, any amount of
'em. Some woman."

He turned about slowly, and looked out
of the opening where the road came up,
into the moonlight. Then he glanced at
the horses, then at the fire, where Laskins

still snored, and the Mexican still crouched in a black heap by his side. Something as near a sigh as the Giant had known for many a year escaped him. With a last look at Pete, who had not moved, he walked slowly toward the fire.

" 'T aint no use," he said.

He sat down opposite the Mexican, who was looking all the while into the embers. A half-hour went by in perfect silence, save for the breath of the night air in the pines. Again the Giant arose and walked noiselessly to the rock. Pete's head had turned a little to the side, and his form had relaxed. The Giant stooped and heard his regular breathing. He had gone to sleep, in spite of the thing that hung in his mind.

The Giant re-crossed the little park, and sat down by the fire, watching the embers. The Mexican had not moved, but sat opposite. Perhaps ten minutes they sat thus, facing each other. The perspiration was thicker on the Giant's brow now. His lips twitched, and his eyes looked a little haggard. As for Lebi his silence was inscrutable. He might have been likened to some silent vulture waiting. Presently it seemed to the Giant that he must speak or cry out. The silence was ghastly.

"They're both asleep," he whispered to the Mexican, eyeing him across the fire.

Lebi nodded.

The Giant waited another minute. He was actually trembling, and two drops of cold perspiration ran down his forehead. He clenched his fists, struggling to keep his composure before the Mexican.

"Which one?" he whispered.

Lebi pointed his finger at Laskins.

Again the Giant sat silent. His face was hot and cold by turns. God! he must end this or shriek out into the night. What devil had entered him—him, the always cool—at this, one of the smallest of his many deeds? God! somehow he had not thought it would be anything like this. Finally he shook his head at Lebi and whispered:

"No—I'll take Laskins!"

Lebi silently demurred. The Giant grew hot, and whispered again with feverish hoarseness:

"You cussed Mexican—take Pete—I won't—God! I won't—you've got to take Pete! Git up!"

A minute more of silence and Lebi arose doggedly, fingering his weapon, and started across the grove toward the rock.

"At the last note o' the whistle!" whispered the Giant, and himself stiffly arose.

He stood near Laskins, whose breathing was still deep and regular, and watched the Mexican nearing the rock. He could make out Pete's form, stretched in sleep in the moonlight. He found himself trembling violently, scarcely able to get his revolver from his belt. The perspiration was oozing from his face, cold and clammy. It was several minutes after he saw the Mexican stop, ready at the rock, before he finally passed a hand across his eyes and stooped over the sleeping figure by his side—still watching Lebi.

Meanwhile the Mexican had reached the rock, stooped, and felt Pete's breath come and go against his cheek. The shadow of the pine finger was just across his mouth now, and waved over the full

lips. One of his hands was still clenched.
His sleep seemed light. The Mexican
placed the muzzle of his weapon close to
the sleeper's temple and waited. His hand
did not shake.

The first three notes of the signal came
low and clear across the grove, and Pete
stirred a little in his sleep. The longer
note, an octave lower, was accompanied
by two shots, almost simultaneous, and the
silence of the night remained as before.

III

The evening breeze from the prairie
was blowing about the little adobe hut
and there were remnants of a gorgeous
sunset over the mesas. The old Frenchman had wandered out and milked the
cow, thrown some hay to the horses in
the adobe stable, and was now standing
by the kitchen stove watching the woman
cook chile. The boy had picketed his
horse a little farther away for the night
than it had been picketed for the day, spent
a few moments in imitating coyotes down
the meadow, howled a little on his own

account because everything else seemed so still, called the dogs after him, and returned to the house. Presently it would be night.

There was a little high window opposite the kitchen door, looking out to the rear along the trail toward the mountains. The old Frenchman, being tall, was the only member of the family who could see anything through it, other than the remnants of sunset. He stood, with the never-absent stoop of his high shoulders, facing the window. His hands were in his pockets, and he occasionally transferred his gaze from the chile to the trail without, absent-mindedly.

There came two spots over the last rise at the horizon. The immovable old man made no remark, but calmly watched. The two spots grew larger and became two horses with riders, trotting the dull, slow trot of the prairies. A quarter of an hour and they were near enough for John's prairie-trained French eye to recognize them. Still he looked calmly out and said nothing. The woman busied herself about the stove, and the boy played with the dogs in the dining-room under the

table. There was something like a large bag
tied across the horse, in front of each rider,
with stiff ends not so much hanging down
as protruding on each side. On coming
closer the bags became blankets with contents well wrapped up.

The dogs both being occupied under
the table, the approach of the travelers
attracted the attention only of the long
Frenchman. The two drew up behind
the house, not being able to see through
the window, thinking themselves unno-
ticed. The Giant dismounted, and the
Mexican followed his example. The two
horses were tied to the post of an almost
extinct corral, only a few yards from the
window. The two riders stopped and
talked close together a moment and seemed
to parley, pointing to the house. In a
moment they walked stolidly round the
end of the hut, the Giant leading the way.
Meanwhile the horses stood with drooped
heads—the stiff things still across their
backs.

" O, it 's you, is it ? " said the Frenchman, with his slow drawl and in no particular tone of voice, as the Giant's huge

form loomed outside the door. The Giant
stooped and entered, and Lebi followed.
Maggie said a hasty " *Com'esta?* " and kept
at her work, eyeing the men now and then
with no excess of good grace.

The Mexican took a drink from the
water-bucket and went out and sat on the
wood-pile with his knees up close to his
face.

" Come into the front room a minute,
can't you, John? " said the Giant, leading
the way without further hesitation. The
old man followed leisurely. They passed
through the dining-room, where the boy
eyed them curiously, on into the so-called
sitting-room—a name brought out of a
dimly remembered better civilization.
They sat down, and the old man stretched
out his long legs, with the trousers caught
up over the backs of his shoes, calmly lit
his pipe, and smoked, looking with no expression at the Giant.

" It 's done, John," said the Giant.

" Yes, I see," said John between puffs,
in his almost gentle, quiet voice.

" We—we did n't have no trouble."

The Frenchman smoked on, settling

himself more comfortably and at fuller length in his chair.

"Lord, though, it was n't the most comfortable job I ever done, somehow," continued the Giant. The Frenchman still watched him with no particular expression of countenance.

"They 're out there," said the Giant presently, pointing with his thumb.

"I seen 'em," replied the Frenchman.

"Carryin' one apiece," continued the Giant, after several minutes. The Frenchman silently puffed out clouds of smoke.

"Well wrapped up," said the Giant.

The two sat still for quite a while.

"John," said the Giant, "it 's a long piece to Wagon Mountain."

"Yes," said the Frenchman; "a pretty long piece."

"Mus' be thirty mile, ain't it, John?"

"Twenty-six, seven."

"Seems twice that long in the night."

Still the Frenchman puffed calmly at his pipe.

"Lord, John," said the Giant suddenly, "I could n't stand it!"

"Stand what?"

"Ridin' with him that way all night."

The Frenchman smiled the large, calm smile that somehow made use of his huge French nose, and puffed away.

"There's something got into my nerves, John—I could n't stand it. Seein' him in front that way, with the moon on him—Lord! I'd see him plainer 'n if there was n't no blanket."

"Which one?"

"Pete."

"Swap, then."

"No, the cussed Mexican shan't touch him. Besides, it 'd be the same with him wrapped up; it 'd be Pete anyhow in the night that way!"

John made no answer.

"Can't do it, John. I 'd do it devilish quick—but Lord! all night, an' the moon, an' the prairies dead as graveyards, an' the coyotes screamin' like dyin' babies— Lord!"

"Want to stay here, eh?"

"We could put 'em out in the stable."

"You know I ain't nothin' to do with this thing, and do n't in no ways approve."

"I know it, John, but a tough old hoss

like you ain't goin' to stand on cere-
monies. Besides, it's the order o' the
law."

" It 's a rotten piece of business."

" Lord, it 's all rotten."

The Frenchman thought a moment.

" Well, it ain't nothin' to me. I 've
slept with 'em worse 'n that. It 's the old
woman. She 'd raise a heap of trouble—
she 's sensitive."

" Maybe she won't find it out—jus' till
early mornin', John—jus' till the sun
clears the ungodly moonshine a little.
Anyhow, you can talk her around. I
can't go on, John—I can't, honest."

They were silent for a little while, the
Frenchman meditating.

" You can talk her around, John."

After a few moments more of meditation the Frenchman slowly arose, stretched
his stiff legs, knocked the ashes out of his
pipe, and swung himself out to the
kitchen. He stood for some time talking
to his wife in a low voice.

Meanwhile the night had descended,
and the early moon, already a little above
the horizon, was pouring yellow light

across the meadow and the prairies. The horses, standing back of the kitchen window, cast long shadows.

Maggie had left the paralytic asleep in his room on the other side of the kitchen. No one heard him walking unsteadily across the floor in his stocking feet, wandering about the room, fumbling at the outer door, going out into the night. The night breezes caught the white gown and fluttered it about his thin legs. His wrinkled old hands were stretched out, nervously groping; his white hair and beard glistened in the moonlight as he tottered, muttering to himself, round the end of the house. He stood a moment, his form bent, his paralyzed brain trying to recall its forgotten purpose. His eye lit at last upon the horses. The moonlight disclosed their unusual burdens. Unsteadily the old man tottered toward them.

John, inside, was startled as he heard his voice close beneath the window, mumbling and guttural: " Whuzz'a—whuzz'a— whuzz'a—", the old blasted interrogatory.

The Frenchman stood for a moment, unable to tell whence the sounds came.

Then both he and Maggie darted out of the door and started round the hut. They had but turned the first corner when a hoarse scream startled the stillness. They came to the spot where he stood, half fallen against one of the horses; clutching the blanket away from the body, so that the moonlight fell on the face, the full lips, the hole in the temple; gasping out a pitiable torrent of insane sobs and broken words; clutching his white hair with his thin hand; staring wild-eyed at the face; and still again screaming hoarsely.

At last, the first time in many days, he uttered coherent words. The intense realization of the fact burst the bond that held his tongue:

" My son! my son! my son!—God! —God!"

The darkness settled over his mind again. He tottered back and circled about, dazed, mumbling to himself in sobs like a shivering child :

" Whuzz'a—whuzz'a—whuzz'a—"

They took him by the arms and led him back. The Giant, who had come to the corner of the house, stepped back from before him, and, when the three had disappeared within, sat down on the ground in the shadow of the hut and held his head in his hands. The Mexican had not moved. He was crouched on the wood-pile, with his knees up close to his face.

The Frenchman and his wife were still quieting the old man within, when the Giant arose and went to the Mexican and whispered huskily:

"That's the end of it!"

"Que?"

"That's the end of it—no more—not another step! I'm goin' back to the mountains!"

"Me no coward," muttered the Mexican, his black eyes glittering.

"I believe you're the devil—cussed if I don't believe you're the devil!" still whispering.

"Me no coward."

"Nor I'm no hound of a coyote! It ends here—not another touch o' them bodies—me ner you neither—I tell you the thing ends here! Come on!"

The Mexican was silent a moment.

"Me no care," he said presently, and

the two started for the horses. The Giant, however, was stopped by John's voice calling him. After some hesitation he reluctantly entered the house.

The old man was lying down, still mumbling to himself. Maggie's eyes were flashing fire, but John's never-to-be-disturbed calm remained the same. For several minutes the Giant stood and looked at the white head on the pillow. It was all he could do to keep from breaking through the door and running into the night. He shifted restlessly.

"You swear you never knowed it?" said John presently.

"I swear it, John—Lord, I do! I never knowed—I never dreamed of it!"

Maggie smoothed the pillow and said nothing, and the boy crept in and crouched on the floor. Several minutes more went by.

"You ain't goin' to Wagon Mountain?" queried John.

"I'm done with it—now an' forever! No, sir—I ain't goin' a step. The money 'd burn my hand!"

The Frenchman struck a light and slowly lit his pipe.

" We'll put 'em in yonder on some beddin' to-night, and in the mornin' we'll bury 'em decent."

A few minutes more of silence, with the old man still mumbling, and John said :

" Come on."

The two men went round the hut. Neither horses nor burdens were visible. Running back to the corner of the house, a dim spot far away toward the prairies on the Wagon Mountain trail told the course of the Mexican.

" The cussed black devil !" cried the Giant after a moment's speechless silence.

The Frenchman puffed a long cloud of smoke into the moonlight.

" Like a Mexican," he said calmly.

" Rottenest set o'·people on God's earth," muttered the Giant, "worse 'n niggers, I'll be cussed !"

AT THE PASSING OF SESCA

T HESE things happened in the old days, some years after John had buried his first wife, and before Maggie came out of the East.

"All alike—sheep-herders," said the long Frenchman. "They get stupid, somehow, kind o' diffused-like in the head. It's bein' with 'em so much all alone that makes 'em queer. They get just like the sheep, for all the world."

He was milking the long-horned cow in the corral back of the adobe house, and the sun was setting behind the mesas. Beside him, leaning against a post, stood the young man from the East.

"You 've never been sorry you took him and Sesca, I suppose?"

"Sorry? Lord, no, Howard; only wished I could make him ever come down.

It ain't good for him up there with nothin'
but the sky and the sheep.   And Sesca—"
He paused in his milking and looked across
the bare brown earth to the hut.   " Sesca
—why, she's been most ever'thing to an
old man like me."

" She's an angel !" said Howard, half
to himself, and turning about restlessly to
walk to and fro.   The old man heard the
exclamation, but made no reply, and calmly
proceeded with his work.

A young girl came round the end of
the house with a basket upon her arm.
She was bare-headed, and the breeze blew
her dark hair gently about her face.   She
came along the path, which passed the corral and ascended the steep rugged sides of
the mesa.   Howard advanced eagerly to
meet her.

" Can't I go with you ?" he said ; " I
want to be with you !"

" No, no," she replied; " not this time.
Let me go alone—I want tell him alone.
Oh !" with a hopeless sigh; " I so afraid !"
Her voice held the accent that had be-
longed to her mother—Spanish.   Indeed
there was much of the Spaniard in her,

displaying itself chiefly in the depth of the
eyes and the dark shade of the hair. Her
face, however, showed a whiteness not be-
longing to the typical Spanish face. It was
relieved by a faint flush of pink when she
spoke.

She started on up the path, Howard's
eyes following her. He was not much
more than a boy, and there was the extreme ardor of youth in his gaze. Some
anxiety was mingled with it, too, and once
he started after her, but halted again and
hesitated, and finally returned.

" Oh ! " he said with anxious impatience; " I don't want her to have to en-
dure it alone. John," abruptly, " why in
the world can't a fellow do everything he
wants to for a woman ? He always has
to stop short and see her go on alone.
There 's a barrier that a man can't pass ;
she 's that much beyond him—in a rarer
atmosphere, somehow."

" Lord, now, you could n't do no good
up there."

" No, of course not. That 's what
hurts."

" Natural, though," said the old Frenchman meditatively, "for you to think that way—restless-like."

Howard's eyes still followed the figure up the path. He sighed.

"I wish—pshaw! there's any amount of things I wish, John."

"Wishin' 's a pleasin' pastime," said the Frenchman, starting slowly toward the house with the milk, moving stiffly. Howard followed him.

"Angel, eh?" said John.

"You know it yourself, John."

The two entered the adobe kitchen, where Nito, the old Mexican cook, with her hair hanging about her swarthy face, was cooking supper. As they did so there were wafted down from the far heights of the mesa faint notes of halting music from the old shepherd's flute, of poor quality, and quavering, but not without sweetness. The tones came gently over the rocks, broken by the intermittent breezes. Howard stood a moment in the door, as he had often done, and listened. It was a small part of an old Moorish air, somewhat wild, and very sad, bringing up repeatedly on a long, plaintive, descending note, with something of languor in it and something of despair.

Sesca's path lay straight up the mesa, very rugged. The mesa at this point rises six hundred feet above the valley. At a little distance its sides seem precipitous, but on climbing one finds them only steep, save near the top. Here a cliff rises abrupt to the summit for fifty feet, and would seem to baffle progress. A fissure, however, visible only on close approach, lets the climber through, up a narrow, uneven stairs of rock to the top.

Long practice had accustomed the girl to the exercise. Yet she must needs stop at times and rest the basket on a rock, or seat herself by the rugged way and look back. The mesas over across the valley were dropping lower as she ascended. The hut far below seemed but a very tiny affair of dull brown in the lighter brown of the valley, and its streamer of smoke fainted in the effort to rise as high as she, seemingly before it had started. Only the mountains beyond and the sunset red over them retained their due proportions. The air was very pure and clear, and the evening breezes were even stronger here, blowing her hair about her face and cooling the flush of her cheeks.

Sitting on a huge rock more than half way up, Sesca could hear the notes of the Moorish air through the stillness. They seemed to come from very high, away up in the thin atmosphere, and Sesca's face saddened as she heard. For a moment she rested her head upon her arms across the basket.

"O,—it will not do!" she murmured.

She arose again and continued the ascent, the broken notes sounding now louder, now fainter, as a dallying breeze brought them to her, or a mass of rock shut them away. She entered at last the fissure, climbed the stairs, and came out upon the summit, where the notes came clear and plaintive across the flat.

The mesa was several miles in circumference, like a level and desolate island high up in a clear sea of air and sky. Its surface was broken by a few rocks, and it was fringed about the island shores with a thin growth of ragged pines.

All the center was bare and brown, the sparse grass failing to relieve the color.

The old shepherd sat upon a low stone close to the ground, with one knee bent up and his ancient flute to his mouth. His dress was old and worn and uncouth. His fingers upon the instrument were dark and wrinkled. Minute wrinkles, too, covered the swarthy, weather-beaten face, from which and about which hung a ragged beard, black and long. He stared before him across the backs of many sheep that grazed over the brown soil, his aspect partaking of the wildness of the air he played. Several sheep stood close about him, and one old, wrinkled ram lay at his feet.

As Sesca approached he ceased his playing and turned his face toward her. There came a sort of light into his eyes, a light of recognition, no doubt of pleasure, but his face was still blank enough, and there was no smile. There was something of the expression of a child about his features, and something, too, of wildness. She went to him without speaking and took

his hand, and passively he arose and was
led by her to a little tent that stood beneath
a pine at no great distance. Before this,
upon a cloth on the dry soil, she spread a
small repast from the basket and seated
him upon a stone beside it. She, herself, sat upon the ground. The old man
ate intermittently and sparingly, watching
the sheep in an absent way, and following
their movements with his eyes. Two or
three of them had come closer and stood
several yards away, stupidly looking on.
The girl ate nothing, but was lost in
thought, and uneasy.

"Father," she said at last, "I—I want
tell you something."

The old man turned his face toward her.
Something in the tone of her voice awakened surprise in him. She caught the
new light in his eyes and crept up closer
to him, with her face white, and suddenly
bent her head upon her hands and sobbed.
Childlike wonder, not unmixed with sorrow, came into his eyes. Hesitatingly the
wrinkled hand arose and passed over her
hair.

"Howard, father—Howard—" she said, not raising her head, "you know him—he has been here—you remember—"

"I know, Sesca—I know," he replied, perhaps something of apprehension displaying itself in the low monotone of his voice.

"He want take me 'way, father."

Still she did not raise her head. The hand ceased to pass over her hair, and was still, across her shoulder. The old man sat without a motion. The seconds going by, her sobs ceased because of the fear for him. Still his hand lay motionless, and she suddenly raised her head and saw his face. There was no sorrow nor reproach in it. He was staring away at the sheep with his eyes wide, and the wild, lost look strangely exaggerated. She threw her arms about his neck passionately, and sunk her face upon his breast.

"O, papa—papa—papa!" she cried, "don't look so—don't look so! I love him so much—so much; and surely you can go!"

He was still staring wildly at the sheep. The flock was by slow degrees coming

closer. After a minute his eyes returned
to the fleecy forms near him, then to the
edge of her dress spread upon the ground,
then to her hair; and, as though recollect-
ing, he began to pass his hand to and fro
over the dark tresses.

"I go?" he said blankly after a
moment.

"Why not, father—why not?" she
cried, raising her face to his. "Tell me
you will go! The East, papa, all the big
East. How much we used talk of it!
How much I wanted go there—away from
where it so lonesome. Tell me you go!
I not want to leave you."

He looked about blankly again, saw the
old flute lying on the ground by him, and
picked it up as though to play, but laid it
down again with a helpless air, and stared
at the sheep.

"We go together, we three. O—he
love me so—he not can leave me! You
will go!"

He still stared about—at the little weather-
blackened tent, at the ragged pines, at the
clear sea of sky with the shadows of night
coming slowly into it, at the rocks and the

brown earth, and at the sheep; the wildness still in his eyes.

"The sheep, Sesca," he muttered.

"Yes, yes—I know. Uncle John take good care of them. He promise. He take, O, such good care!"

He stared at her.

"Why—why—" he said, "leave 'em, Sesca?—You do n't mean leave 'em!"

She saw the hopelessness of it, and laid her head again upon his shoulder.

"Leave 'em, Sesca? Why—I can't— I can't!" with a despairing wail in the words. "Why, Sesca, what 'd they do?"

That contained it all—his life. What could they do without him? Some of them were close to him now, and he rubbed the white fleece of one and called its name and stared blankly at it.

She arose and walked aimlessly about, and returned and put her arms about his neck and wept, then walked away again and looked wet-eyed at the distant mountains. Absently the shepherd took the flute and started the old air, but ceased in the middle; and after a pause started it again, and ceased again.

Howard's face suddenly appeared at the opening in the cliff. Seeing Sesca's grief, he guessed her failure, and hastened to her.

"I could n't stay," he said. "I guessed this. I was afraid. I do n't know what I can do, but I wanted to try."

"It not any use, Howard," she said. He kissed her gently, and she sank down on the ground where she was, and waited.

The old man was still watching the sheep with a dazed expression. His elbows were on his knees as he sat on the rock, and his chin rested on his hands, one of which held the flute. Howard approached and stood before him.

"Won't you go with us?" he said. "We want you — Sesca needs you. It will not be well for you here alone; I do not think you can stand it at all."

After a pause the shepherd spoke.

"But the sheep," he said, with his eyes wandering over them.

Howard watched them too, and turned from them to Sesca, weeping yonder on the ground, and back again to the shepherd. He had seen the strength of this before. Finally the old man's silence was again broken. He began speaking in his dull monotone, somewhat as though to himself.

" Sesca — Sesca — " he said. " I 've had her all alone, ever since she was jus' such a little thing. Since her mother died. Used to be she 'd set on my knee of a night. Hair always black like that — Spanish, after her mother, an' talk Spanish-like. I never thought o' nothin' like this — never thought. Then, when she got bigger, always helpin' round perty an' fresh-like. Then when we come here, ever' evenin' this way — was n't no use to go down — jus' Sesca an' the sheep. Ever' evenin'. Why — why — what 'll I do ! " a little wildly again; " what 'll we do — me an' the sheep ! "

" Come with us — you won't have to bear it. It will be so much better with us ! "

" Leave the sheep ? Why — no, you do n't know ! Why, I *can't !* Look at 'em there now — look at him with his old wrinkled horns, and them yonder, and this young one here. Leave 'em ? I can't — I can't ! "

The last words were a pitiful cry, and

the despair in them showed Howard the uselessness of his appeal. He turned away with a criminal feeling in his heart.

"It has come to the decision, Sesca," he said, as they stood apart on the path, with the last glow of the sun behind them. He turned away from her, that no expression of his might influence her.

At last she went to her father, who still sat on the rock with the silent flute in his hands. She threw her arms about his neck again and cried for a moment. Gathering up the contents of the basket, she returned, and the two started to descend. At the fissure of rocks Howard pressed her close to him with his heart beating swiftly, as they turned for the last time. The shepherd was still seated in the dusk, staring across the backs of the sheep. With a pitiful little cry Sesca turned away, Howard still supporting her with his arm, feeling the tremor of her sobs, his own heart aching for her. He longed to lift her and carry her down — away — out of it all.

On the descent Sesca was weak with grief. Half-way down she gave way and sank upon a stone. Howard knelt beside her, covering her face with kisses.

"It's too much for you—too much!" he cried passionately. "O Sesca, my darling, why can't I bear it for you?"

"I bear it," she sobbed, "I bear it. Only—only—O Howard, so much I love you both! It break my heart!"

He held her closer and kissed the lips and white forehead. She was quieter at last, and the tears were dried.

"The stage come to-morrow morning; is it not?"

"To-morrow; yes."

"I want go then—I not stay longer!"

It was quite dark when they came at last to the house, though there were hints of the coming moon in the east. As they came over the last stretch of the path, there floated down from the mesa the faint tones of the Moorish air—but more halting and intermittent.

The old Frenchman, with his pipe in his mouth, and his never-absent stoop of the high shoulders, awaited them at the wood-pile.

"Just lookin' at the moonshine over

there and listenin' to the horses pawin' in the stable," he said, half apologetically. His calm old eyes, however, observed them narrowly.

The three entered the house in silence. In silence, also, the old Mexican put the supper on the table, and silently they ate. Howard was depressed and abstracted. Sesca's face still held the traces of tears, showing in the lamplight, and she ate but little. John watched them calmly by turns, and meditated with no change of expression in his never-varying features. Old Nito ate busily. In silence still they arose.

John walked stiffly into the so-called front room, and lit his pipe and sat himself down in the large chair and smoked. Howard went out into the night, and walked to and fro along the stage-road restlessly. Some of the light from the dining-room shone in upon the Frenchman, and was lighting the smoke as it curled from his pipe, when Sesca came in. She walked aimlessly about the room, touching and arranging little things here and there, while John's eyes followed her. Presently she went to him and knelt on the floor

with her head on his knee. Gradually
the pipe went out.

"Uncle John?"

"What is it, Sesca?"

"You think I do wrong?"

"To leave him up there, Sesca?"

"Yes."

The Frenchman sighed.

"He could n't go, Sesca—I knew it.
Such as him would n't know anything
about leavin'. Why, it 'd be most like
comin' to die, to him."

"I knew it—I knew it! O, I so was
afraid!"

"But he'll be all right, Sesca."

"I do n't know. I afraid not. He
love me so much."

The Frenchman looked out at the lamp
in the next room, and at the dishes and
the empty chairs.

"Yes," he said; "he loves you—Lord,
we all love you."

"But you know I can't help to go,
Uncle John—you know."

"I know, Sesca."

"You think I do not right?" still with
her head on his knee.

"No, no, child, it—why, yes, it's right." After a pause, "It's all right, Sesca."

"We must go in the morning, Uncle John."

The old man meditated a while on this, looking at her hair. He took a lock of it between his stiff fingers and curled it about them.

"Well," he said calmly, at last, "I reckon it's best."

There was a long silence, and the pipe dropped from his hand and fell upon the floor.

"Uncle John?"

"What is it, Sesca?"

"You—you miss me some, Uncle John?"

"Lord, Sesca, yes—yes; we'll miss you. But an old man like me can—can stand it. Just an old man like me. And we're glad to see you happy, you know, Sesca."

"You been so good to me—so good! I not ever forget!"

He still fondled the lock of hair and said nothing.

" Uncle John ? "

" Yes, Sesca."

" I know you take such good care of him—for me, Uncle John."

" I promise it, Sesca—Lord, yes; I promise it. Ever'thing I can do, honey; do n't never be afraid of that."

At last she arose and he kissed her and watched her as she went out. Then he found his pipe again and lit it and smoked.

At ten o'clock they were all in bed, the packing having been done. Sesca occupied the front room, John and Howard slept on cots in the dining-room, and Nito was alone in the room beyond the kitchen. John could not sleep, and the restless pawing of one of the horses in the adobe stable across the trail annoyed him. He feared the animal had effected some damage, and arose and dressed himself, and went out. The moon was up now, and shining brightly, and the night was very white and still. He found the horse entangled in its rope, and was occupied some minutes in releasing it. He came out of the stable again, and stood for a moment in the trail.

There came suddenly to his ears the sound of the flute from the mesa, plain through the still air. He was startled that it seemed nearer than was its wont. This time the Moorish phrase, still plaintive and somewhat wilder, reached the long descending note, and the despair of the tone wailed among the rocks up the mesa's side. John started in a walk, unusually fast for him, along the mesa path. The flute-notes seemed nearer and nearer as he approached. At last he broke into a run, and began the steep ascent.

He could descry the figure, a black spot high above him, in the moonlight. A quarter of the way up, and the tones were close at hand. John stopped to breathe, against a rock. The path was very narrow and rugged here, and dim in the night. Somehow the shepherd had lost it, and John could see him only a little distance away, coming down the side of the mesa, over the roughness of untraveled rocks. His gait was perilous. His eyes, even in the moonlight, shone wide and wild. The night breeze blew the black beard and hair about his face.

He held the flute to his lips, and was playing the despairing notes over and over again.

The mesa before him sloped to the top of a boulder a dozen feet high, which the path wound about. John saw the danger, and with a great leap of his long limbs started across the broken space between. The madman still came on. In a moment more he had tripped and fallen over the ledge to the path beneath. When John came to the spot, he was lying in a black heap, with his face up, and on his forehead a cut from a sharp rock was oozing blood. The flute was still clutched in his hands, but broken.

The Frenchman knelt beside him and tried to arouse him, but the shepherd was unconscious. After a moment of rest, John lifted the body in his arms, and carried it laboriously down the mesa and along the path to the house. He came to the outside door of Nito's room, the one farthest away from the rest of the house, and knocked gently. Nito was finally aroused without noise, and made to dress and open the door.

"Be just as still as you know how," said John, entering with his burden.

The woman lit a lamp. She was well-nigh overcome with stupid surprise, though still blinking with sleep.

"He fell down the mesa. Get the old cot ready there, and we'll put him on it."

She obeyed, and the old man was stretched out, John bending over him anxiously.

"No dead," said the Mexican.

"Sure?"

"Me sabe too much 'bout dead people. Him no dead."

"No, I don't think he's dead."

The shepherd opened his eyes and stared glassily a moment, and sighed and closed them again.

"Sort o' faint—'s all," said John. "Now you want to keep mighty still—hear?" He turned about almost fiercely, facing her in the light of the lamp, and emphasized the order with a gesture of his hand.

"Keep them doors shut tight and locked—now and in the mornin'. 'T ain't likely they'll want to come in—but they sha'n't if they want. He 'll most likely be perfectly still. And do n't you so much as open your mouth about his bein' here. Mind you—they ain't to know it—Sabe? "

His meaning began to dawn on the Mexican.

" Me sabe. Me keep mum," she said.

The old man was up early in the morning, as indeed were the others. While Sesca and Howard were finishing preparations for departure and Nito was cooking breakfast, John went into Nito's room.

He came out again after a few moments, calmly locked the door, put his hands in his pockets, and went to feed the horses, smoking and meditating. Breakfast was almost as silent a meal as the supper had been. John tried once in an ineffectual way to say something to cheer the party up, and Sesca made a very weak show of being sure they would come back before long to see them all again. At last the four-horse stage came rattling over the stony trail from the west and drew up at the well.

" I brought your cape out of Nito's

room, Sesca," said John, standing about awkwardly watching the final preparations. "I guess you 've got ever'thing you kept in there. Got all your things now?"

"All, I think, Uncle John. Good-by, Nito," said Sesca, taking the swarthy hands, the tears beginning to show in her eyes. "Good-by, Uncle John—good-by—good-by!" almost in sobs now. "O—you so good to me! I not ever forget!"

They were seated, and John had hugged her close at the step of the stage and lifted her in, and taken Howard's hand in his own horny one, and said a last "God bless you both!"

Sesca's last look was toward the top of the mesa, with its jagged rocks against the morning sky; and as the stage disappeared in the distance they saw her arms about her lover's neck and knew that she was sobbing with her head upon his shoulder.

Nito started slowly into the house. The old man stood by the well and lit his pipe and puffed the smoke into the still morning air. At last he turned and entered the kitchen. His eyes wandered about the room.

" Different, somehow," he said,—" all sort o' different. Well," after a pause, " just an old man like me."

He puffed in silence for a moment more.

" Was n't no use bein' afraid of him in there attractin' their attention, Nito."

Nito stopped in her work and turned about and looked at John and then at the door of her room.

" He 's dead," said the Frenchman.

THE RACE

❧

O N a day of much sunshine and southern breeze a mixed crowd of some
four or five hundred persons, male
and female, went out of the little town,
climbed a rise in the southern trail that led
away yonder into the blue sky, and gathered at the scene of the coming race. The
course was a straight one of three
hundred yards, measured out at haphaz-
ard in the flat of the prairie. There had
never been a race just here before, and probably would never be a race just here again;
but the " cowhorses " were matched, and
the thing was to be done. The town was
left to shift for itself, as dead as the deserted homes of the cliff-dwellers. Half
the men were galloping about on mus-
tangs, the brims of their sombreros flap-
ping in the wind, their coiled lassos
dangling from the saddle-horns.

Others of the men, and some of the

women, were on foot, covered with dust, red of visage, but more jovial than anything that can be seen east of the western Kansas line. Here and there vehicles of doubtful age and pattern stood or wandered about—perhaps one two-seated carriage bearing evidences of past gentility and seemingly distressed at the happenings of its old age ; even "South Bend" wagons alongside of prairie-schooners, dogcarts, and spring-wagons. The noise, the uproarious laughter, the red-faced shouting of bets, the tossing of money, joined in the making of confusion.

Riding slowly down the course came a small man upon a raw-boned, gaunt, roan animal. The man was bare-headed, with loose, unkempt hair straggling about his ears. His face was full-cheeked, with weak eyes, jovial expression, and a complexion well-nigh flaming. His horse was one of the racers, and he himself was to ride it, as was evidenced by his lack of shoes, his stockinged feet being thrust into the loops of a rope passed over the horse's back. These served for stirrups, there being no saddle.

"Hey!" yelled the rider, in a blaring voice, and rolling his eyes in jocose acknowledgment of his wit. "Hey! you feller, you 're bettin', ain't you? I 'll bet you ten dollars this hoss can't run his best!"

There was a roar of laughter from the crowd, and a volley of responses.

"I 'll bet he can't drink all he can swaller!"

"Him? That there hoss ain't wuth a plaster-paris dollar!"

"Do n't you fool yourself—by thunder, he jis' gits down and slides!"

Another rider came up and met the first.

"Jim, you goin' to beat me?" he shouted to the other. A sort of restrained smile came into his eyes, which were so extremely near together that a burly by-stander cried:

"That there feller's eyes both comes out o' the same hole!"

The crowd roared again and thronged about the riders.

"Put up yer money!" cried a lean prospector from the mountains.

" Twenty dollars on the roan! " shouted
a Mexican, passing a bill over the heads of
the people.

" A dollar and a half fer the bay! "

" Fifty cents to yer boots it 's a tie! "

Meanwhile Jim looked at his compet-
itor.   In the very narrow space between
the black eyes of the latter his nose seemed
long and thin.   It was also a trifle red.
His complexion was sallow.   He wore a
tattered sombrero, the half of a pair of
suspenders, no coat, hat, nor shoes.

" Goin' to beat me, eh? " he said good-
humoredly.

" Well, now, I 'm goin' to break myself tryin', Cal," said Jim.

" This here bay hoss o' mine, you know,
Jim, ain't no 'count."

" What you stuffin' at me?   Ain't I
seen him? "

" Yes, but he moves queer.   If he beats
it 's because his lef' hine leg an' his right
front one is gone wrong an' moves too
irregular fast fer to be doin' right, an' jist
gits him over the ground in spite of hisself.   He can't help it.   Haw! haw! "
He laughed hoarsely at the joke, and the

crowd laughed with him. He turned and started slowly toward the upper end of the course, saying:

" Well, Jim, ain't it about time to let out? "

Jim watched him a minute curiously and rode after him, saying to the by-standers:

" Ain't Cal a dern jokey sort of a fel-ler? "

Half-way up the course there stood among the rest of the people a very slim but very boisterous girl, with small blue eyes, stringy light hair, and a faded, dusty dress. She was waving her arms in a more or less sheepish manner, and shout-ing in a shrill voice:

" Hurrah fer the roan! "

" He ain't goin' to beat," said a grin-ning cowboy next her.

" Well, I reckon he is! " said the girl. " Gee! I'll be broke up if he do n't. I 'm jist all of a tremble."

" Nell's gittin' worked up," said one of the bystanders.

At this moment Jim came riding by on his way to the upper end of the course.

"Jim! Jim!" shrieked the girl, her tones thin and rasping, as she waved a dusty hat a little doubtfully at him. "Go at it, Jim! You're goin' to have 'em all crazy!"

Jim turned his face toward her, rather startled. Somehow the thing did not seem to please him. He scowled and looked ahead at Cal, and went on, saying nothing.

"That's the feller you're goin' to marry, ain't it?" said the cowboy next her.

"That's what I am," said Nell, sharply.

"When?"

"To-morrow, that's when," said the girl. She was looking after the rider, still doubtfully.

"I wonder what's wrong with him now?" she said to herself.

The riders had reached the head of the straight course of three hundred yards, and were preparing to start.

"Tipsy!" shouted Cal, turning his near-set eyes about upon the crowd. "Where in the devil's Tipsy?"

"Here!" cried a boy's voice, as the boy himself appeared running out of the crowd.

"Fix this here lef' loop, will you? Look at it, it's all gittin' yanked up. It'll be hangin' me over the banisters here before I git his lef' hine leg an' his right front one to workin' in conjugation along with the others!" He winked a large, slow, solemn wink at the boy.

Tipsy was a reckless, happy, ugly, sparkling-eyed little chap. He wore the half of an old sombrero, set back so that the hair hung in one of his eyes, tattered trousers, and shoes too large but not preventing very lively movement.

"There you are!" he cried after fixing the loop. "Now git out an' sail!"

He gave the horse a resounding slap on the hip and backed toward the crowd.

Jim's red face was turned stolidly to the front, and his eyes were fixed on the roan's ears. The roan was champing the bit viciously and throwing his head about. Cal was eyeing Jim, and his smaller bay horse stood still. The start was made from a stand, and by the "one, two, three"

of a starter.   Simultaneously the riders
dug spurs into the horses' sides, leaned far
over the horses' necks, and furiously the
beasts leaped away down the course. The
sandy dust of the prairie rose in a swirled
cloud behind. Already the most of the
crowd had gathered near the lower end,
and at the start they swerved breathless
and in silence, still closer together about
the point of finish. The horses came
over the prairie like birds, stretching themselves out in frantic response to the spurs,
and running neck and neck.

" Go it !   Go it ! " shrieked the thin-
voiced Nell, leaping up and down in un-
gainly excitement, as the beasts hissed by
her. Even in that small moment Jim
found thought to mutter to himself in
deep disgust :

" Listen to that fool gal ! "

At no time in the race was there any
perceptible difference in the speed of the
animals. Jim was plying his spur frantic-
ally, and Cal, leaning far over the bay's
neck, still had his near-set eyes turned
across the course at the roan. A great
yell arose from the crowd, and amid a

whirlwind of dust and a muffled thunder of
hoofs the two horses shot past the point
of finish, so nearly even that a decision was
impossible.

Tipsy came leaping down the course,
yelling shrilly that the bay had beaten by
half a length, though he himself had been
a hundred yards from the finish. Jim rode
back into the shouting crowd, declaring it
was he who had won by a head. Every-
one else had his own opinion, and was mor-
ally and loudly certain of its correctness.

"Jim beat!" cried Nell, hurrying up
breathless and flustered, and coughing
with the dust. "I seen him! He was
clean ten feet ahead, by George! I seen
him! I tell you Jim beat!"

The air was full of similar and con-
verse opinions, opinions yoked in general
by the pressure of the bets. Jim looked
at Nell and turned and spent his argu-
ments on another part of the crowd. Cal
alone sat silent, looking at the people in a
sort of grim amusement. It was finally
decided that the race was a tie.

"Well, then," shouted Jim, "the only
thing to do is to try it agin."

" Come on," said Cal.

The course was retraced, and the stand again taken at the upper end.

" Jim beat, I tell you ! " shrieked the excited Nell. " They ain't no use to run it agin, nohow—he 's done won it oncet ! "

" Aw he ain't neither," growled Tipsy, ready for belligerency on the spot, which, however, was prevented by the start.

Once more the horses came down the course. The plying of spurs, the plowing of the foam of sandy earth, the swerving of the crowd, and the final yell, were repeated. A second time, after much vociferous contention, the race was declared a tie.

" Well," said Jim, his face fairly flaming by this time, " then, by thunder, there ain't nothin' to do but run it agin ! "

" Come on," said Cal.

At the third finish the roan, influenced perhaps by unusual poignancy of spur-digs from Jim, perhaps by an extra whoop from the shrill voice of Nell, was clearly half a length ahead. The crowd's shout was fuller and more prolonged. Jim came riding back in boisterous delight. Cal returned calmly.

"He went an' got 'em to workin' too regular," the latter said, winking his long slow wink at the despairing Tipsy. "It was runnin' him three times that way that done it. First two times his lef' hine leg an' his right front one was workin' all wrong, jist gittin' him over the ground so 's he could n't help hisself, an' he come nigh beatin'. But you see they got worked down regular. After another two er three this here hoss 'd git to goin' so blame smooth an' perfeck that it 'd jist be like sleepin' to him."

"I knowed it! I knowed it!" cried Nell, hastening up panting. "M-*hm!*— got beat, did n't you?"

Jim eyed her and turned away. His delight in the victory was short lived. He rode on into town grunting to himself. The crowd, still shouting and laughing, bandied the money about like chaff and finally dispersed. With much galloping of horses, rattling of vehicles, and dust-wading of pedestrians, the course was

left deserted out in the bare middle of the
prairie's nothingness; the trail was traversed, and the town revived.

The town consisted of a schoolhouse,
a very small Methodist church, one little
hotel, six saloons, four or five stores, and
two or three straggling streets of houses,
mostly adobe. As evening came on, a
solitary man sat on a goods box behind
one of the smallest stores, kicking some
empty tomato-cans absently with his foot.
It was Jim. His complexion had lost
little of its splendor. He was still, to
judge from his expression, in an unpleasant
state of mind.

Cal came out of the rear door with his
hands in his pockets, and his customary
calm manner of seeming to feel the humor
of the situation, if there were any. He
eyed Jim out of the eyes that " both came
out of the same hole." Jim looked up.

" Well, Cal," he said, " you ain't broke
up none because I beat you, are you? "

" I told you you never done it. It was
the uncommon regularity o' the hoss's
feet."

" But you ain't kickin' none? "

Cal took a chew of tobacco, and said meditatively:

"Well, no. What kind of a feller do you reckon I am? Did n't you know I was bettin' on your hoss?"

"Thunder!" said Jim.

"Looky here, Jim. Let's git out o' this here place."

"What fer?" said Jim, looking up with something almost like excitement in his weak eyes.

"Why, looky here. There ain't no money here. Now I been racin', foot-racin' an' hoss-racin', ever since I can recollect, an' it's got to be a habit, you know—jist like cussin' er combin' a feller's hair 'll grow on him. Me an' you got the two best hosses anywheres in the territory outside the rings. Let's git to travelin' round an' puttin' up races. We can fix 'em up to suit the bets."

Cal spat into the air, smiled a large, bland smile, and winked his slow wink.

"Can't," said Jim.

"Why?"

"O, I'm goin' to git married to-mor-row."

Cal walked round him a few steps in some calm amazement, eyeing him as he might have eyed a curiosity.

" No! " he said.

" O, the devil! " said Jim, kicking the cans viciously. " It's so—that's what it is! "

Cal looked on with his hands in his pockets. Finally he gave a little internal puff of laughter.

" What on earth did you do it fer, Jim? "

" W'y, *I* do n't know. What a fool a feller is! "

" Got tired of it, eh? "

" O, it's sick'nin'! "

" Who is she? "

" W'y," still irritated, " that there gal —you seen her—there at the race, what they called Nell. *I* do n't know what her other name is—she ain't got none! " He spoke contemptuously.

Cal stood and looked calmly at Jim.

" What's the matter with her? " he said.

" O, she jist makes sich a fool of her-self! "

" H'm! " said Cal in a kind of half-

laugh. He seemed calmly amused, and
the very large smile came blandly over his
face again.

"Well, then," he said, "I do n't see
why you won't come an' go with the
hosses. You talk like you do n't want to
git married. What 's to hinder jist
leavin' ?"

Jim kicked the cans again and said
nothing.

"Jist kind o'—move off, you know,"
said Cal, with his huge wink.

Jim still was silent.

"I can see plain," said Cal, "that
you 're hankerin' that way. I know.
You 're kind o' back'ard about knowin'
how to go at it. It is onhandy, but it
ain't no real trouble after you git into it.
I done it once. Jist go at it cool. Le 's
see. You can't go ridin' off in the day-
time, because any amount of 'em 'd see
you an' wonder where in the devil you
was goin', fer you can see all the way
from four to ten miles all around here.
It 'd be wuss in the night, fer they 'll all be
drunk an' tearin' around all night, 'specially
to-night after the race."

He meditated quite a while, standing with his hands in his pockets and chewing slowly. Jim kicked the cans again, then eyed Cal, then returned to the cans. His face wore the additional redness of internal exertion. At last Cal turned toward him, his small eyes still dreamy with meditation.

"O, it's easy enough," he said, smiling again. "Looky here now."

He cast his eyes about to see that no one was near, sat down on the box beside Jim, marked his plans out on the palm of one hand with the finger of the other, and, in a hoarse whisper, began. Jim seemed dubious at first, but as the explanation proceeded his eyes became wider, finally sparkling with delight. His complexion grew vivid with excitement. When Cal had finished and leaned back, eyeing him with the bland smile, Jim slapped both hands upon his thighs and burst into a roar of laughter. He broke off quite suddenly.

"But look here," he said, "ain't it a devil of a ways?"

"Ain't I a foot-racer?" said Cal in

some scorn. " An' as fer you — why, I
had an idee you 'd think it was wuth it."

Jim broke again into the laugh, uproarious to feverishness.

" Well, by thunder ! I guess it is!" he
said.

" An' as fer the hosses—why, there 's
Tipsy," said Cal.

Later the two walked together up the
principal street. They found Tipsy and
Nell in a store near the schoolhouse
quarreling over the issue of the race. Cal
called Tipsy out and walked away with
him. Jim was now in high spirits. He
laughed excitedly with the girl and the
store-keeper, and finally took Nell off to
the one little hotel to give her " a rousin'
good supper." Jim was amply capable
of playing his part, and the girl's shrill
laughter as they sauntered along together
announced her approval of his conduct.

In the middle of the following morning
Tipsy might have been seen riding past
the Methodist church, which stood at the
very edge of the town, out across the
prairie toward a line of distant mesas some
three or four miles to the west. Tipsy

was whistling shrilly, with his half-sombrero still on the back of his head and his hair in his eye. He was leading two horses behind the one he rode. One of them was a bay, the other a gaunt roan.

About noon those who were to witness the marriage ceremony came and opened the little church and went in. Some nine or ten cowboys came first, among whom was Cal, calmly surveying the surroundings and chewing tobacco. The party sat down on the front benches and awaited the arrival of the principals.

" She's dern ugly," said one with unblushing frankness.

" She ain't no uglier 'n him," said another.

" Well, a man's always ugly. A man's got to be ugly."

" She's so kind o' noisy an' fussy, somehow," put in a third.

" Some fellers is jis' plumb ijjits," said a huge, broad-shouldered giant.

" Wonder what's keepin' 'em so long? "

" Why, the devil, you do n't reckon nobody 's goin' to trot to their weddin', do you? Give 'em time! "

" Fellers," said Cal, finally, winking more to himself than to any one else. " You ain't treatin' this here thing with no right kind o' respeck. You do n't seem in no ways to git onto the solemness. This here, gentlemen, is a weddin'."

Others began to appear. There were two or three old women of the town, chattering volubly ; a couple of young Mexican girls chewing gum and giggling at the cowboys; and the minister's wife, who sat in the rear corner by herself.

Finally the two objects of interest appeared at the door. Jim's face was painfully red, as usual. A stiff collar seemed cutting his throat, and there was perspiration on his forehead. Nell wore the same dress she had worn the day before, and upon it was the same dust. Her light hair distributed itself in irregular wisps about her head, and at places protruded aimlessly into the air. She looked about sharply and tossed her head recklessly. She was in doubt about Jim no more, and was free to observe all the surroundings. The one aisle chanced to be so narrow that the two could not walk side by side.

"Git along first!" said Nell raspingly.

Jim's face grew fiery, and he obeyed, tramping stolidly to the front, his eyes cocked sideways all the while at Cal's calm visage. Nell followed. She was in no wise subdued by the occasion. Cal's face caught her eye and seemed to awaken malice in her. She leaned over the seat nearest him and whispered loudly :

"Got beat, did n't you? H'm! got beat!"

The minister, who had meanwhile entered a small rear door, was somewhat taken aback at this unusual proceeding, but soon regained his presence of mind.

"Here," he said to Nell, who was shifting about feverishly, in some doubt as to the place to stand. "Jes' stand right there. And, mister, you git right along side of her."

There was a good deal of tittering and whispering in the audience. Jim's eyes were still swerved far to the right, fastened upon Cal, who responded with a wink, unusually prolonged, and employing the majority of his features.

The preliminaries were gotten through

within irregular, but seemingly satisfactory style.   There was some hitch at odd times, owing to a lack of knowledge on Jim's part as to whether or not there were anything required of him.   Some   candid promptings from Nell, however, delivered in a manner effective, if not appropriate, bridged over the difficulties.   Cal was smiling his bland smile when the minister came to the words :

"If any man can show just cause why they may not lawfully be joined together, let him speak now, or else hereafter forever hold his peace."

There was a second's silence, and Cal arose. He coughed an introductory cough, and stepped to the front, his face deeply solemn, his hand raised in an attitude such as the minister might have employed in delivering a benediction.

"Well, now," he said in a nasal, querulous, slightly elevated tone, "looky here. I sure put in a kick. This thing ain't smooth ner regular.   Yes, sir—it's me that objects!"

Nell fell back in amazement, the preacher appeared stupefied, and the audience leaned forward in breathless interest. It was Jim upon whom the matter of action devolved, for Cal stood calm and silent. Jim turned squarely about and faced the objector, seemingly in a red frenzy of wrath. Then he rolled his sleeves far up above his elbows and started at him.

" By thunder ! " he yelled furiously, " you git out o' here ! "

In a sort of weak terror, exquisite to behold, Cal backed down the aisle before him, murmuring querulously :

" Well, now—hold on—you do n't give a feller no show."

" You git out ! " roared Jim, bearing down steamingly.

As they approached the door, Cal's terror plainly increased ; he ceased backing, turned, and ran wildly out of the door, with the perspiring Jim in close pursuit.

In a jumble of frantic curiosity and no little wrath, Nell and the audience rushed to the door and out upon the prairie. Far out in the middle of the plain they beheld Cal dashing away to the west, with Jim following hotly. Speechless, Nell stood and watched, her eyes staring stupidly at the retreating

figures, her mouth dropping open in nerveless wonder.   Never a word was said.
Ten minutes went by, and the distant
chase continued, the figures becoming
smaller and smaller against the unvarying
brown of the prairie.   Nell caught her
breath a little and planted her feet and
stared with feverish intensity.   Ten minutes more and the figures had become
specks.   The members of the audience
began to look about blankly at one another.
Still Nell spoke never a word.   A little
longer and the specks were lost in the
misty outline of the distant mesas.   The
men were gone, and the erratic Nell and
the disappointed audience, the town and
its barren vicinity, saw them no more.

HER HOME-COMING

TIMID little Mrs. Serna came out of the hut and crossed the trail to the minute chapel that stood in the garden. She wore over her head a small dull shawl, which hung down about her slim shoulders, and from which her face, with its many small wrinkles, peered meekly. As usual, she carried her hands crossed before her. The worn dress, that had been black, came just below the shoe-tops, and the shoes themselves were brown with age.

The church—her church—was not more than fifteen feet square, made of adobes, and, without, plain to monotony. There was no tower and no vestibule and barely windows. The flat walls arose to meet the flat roof, and the flat roof was earthen, like the walls. It was three miles to another house, and twenty miles to a priest or any one whom little Mrs. Serna could

have felt in her heart to be a good Catholic. There might seem to have been no
use for the little church, for nobody ever
sang in it or preached in it, and the stage-
road passing by knew nothing of worship,
and the mesas about knew it only in their
own inscrutably silent way. But to the
little Mexican woman with the quiet blue
eyes there was use for the church.

A wooden door gave entrance, and Mrs.
Serna pushed it open and went in, and
closed it behind her. There were not
any seats within; the hard earthen floor
was quite bare, and the little room seemed
empty. At the other end, however, was
the altar, and the dim light was reflected
from many a dazzling thing upon it and
around it. The Blessed Mary was there,
and Mrs. Serna knelt before the rude
wooden image, and thought, in the midst
of her prayers, that the paper halo which
she herself had reverently placed upon the
Virgin's brow must be straightened.

There were saints, of wood also, and
painted very strangely, but as well as Mrs.
Serna could do it. The figures were all
small; they were the best she could get,

and large ones would have been too large
for the room and the low ceiling. She
knew very well that it made no difference.

In the center, and higher up, was the
Crucified One, hanging there as He had
hung since she first timidly placed Him
there many years ago. The blood was
painted naturally, she thought—how very
terrible it would be to bleed like that. She
was too meek to have thought it out very
far, but she could kneel down here on the
bare earth of the floor and pray for Cornelio, and Anita, and for those who had
gone—José and Gertie and poor old Lauriano himself; which was all the church
was for.

There was a good deal of tinsel and
pink and gold paper and little pieces of
china about the figures and the altar. She
had done as much of that as she could,
and had tried to make it really pretty and
like what she thought a cathedral would
be. She had never seen a cathedral, for
she had always lived here. But they had
told her about it; and old Lauriano, before
he died, had helped her to decorate the
church. Even on the Christ there was an

odd little paper skirt, which she had changed many times. She was not sure that it was just as it should be. The pink she had thought unsuitable to the blood, and had tried the gold. But she had at length discarded both for the white one of tissue paper, which looked better. Mrs. Serna knelt longer to-day than usual, and a few more tears fell than had been accustomed to fall.

The door behind her opened, and Cornelio came in. He was a short man with an ugly face, but not unkindly eyes. He took off his hat and watched his mother for a while. Apparently she had not heard him.

"Mother," he said presently.

She arose hurriedly, like one caught unawares and confused, and folded her hands.

"It is time to go, you know. We ought to start in half an hour. Anita is waiting already."

"Yes, Cornelio, I was coming." She smoothed the shawl down and looked hopelessly all about the church, from the Blessed Mary to the Christ, and thence to

the walls and the bare floor.   But she
made no move to go out.

"Mother," said Cornelio again, fingering his hat.

"Yes, yes," she said, startled again and
speaking like one frightened.   "I am
coming, Cornelio."

Again Cornelio waited.   He could see
his mother was struggling with herself,
and knowing that she would speak presently, he said no more.   After fluttering
a little and looking about again, the blue
eyes were raised to Cornelio.

"Cornelio," she said, speaking not
much above a whisper, "I can hardly bear
to be going.   It's very much worse than
I thought.   But — never mind; I know
it is right — I can go."   She dropped
her eyes to the floor, fingered the worn
fringe of the shawl, and stepped to the
corner of the church.   "Cornelio," she
said, tapping her foot on the hard earth,
"your father is under this spot here.   Poor
old Lauriano.   It was right here.   He
picked out the spot himself.   And over
here, this is José, just about here, with his
head this way, next to Lauriano.   His feet

come only to about here. Then right here is Gertie — you can remember that yourself. Poor little Gertie. Nobody would know they were here now, would they ? "

She raised the corner of her shawl to her eyes and stood and looked through the fringe at the earth.

" Cornelio."

" Well, what is it, mother ? "

" I 've told you I 'd go with you, Cornelio, because you 've got a big ranch now and more cattle to take care of. At first I could n't bear its being four miles from the church, and even yet it do n't seem like it 's really me that 's going away. It seems like it 's somebody else. But I 'll go ; I 've told you I 'll go. There 's just one thing I want you to promise."

Cornelio fingered his hat and stood and waited. He was growing a little impatient.

" I could n't lie in peace anywhere else," she said. " I could n't go a step if I thought I 'd have to. I 'd die right here to-day. Seems like I 'd rise up in my grave anywhere else. Here 's the place

I 've set — me here, and Lauriano here, and José and Gertie over here. Promise me, Cornelio, promise me honest and true, that whatever comes you 'll bring me back and put me here beside these three.''

Cornelio promised, took out his ancient silver watch and looked at the time, and insisted that now they must go.

By the next day they were fairly settled in the new house four miles away,—Cornelio, his mother, and his sister Anita. This day and nearly all of the days following, Cornelio was gone from morning till night over the prairie that stretched in every direction, on his rounds among the cattle. Mrs. Serna tried the best she could to seem at home, but she had never lived so far away as this.

" Anita,'' she said one morning, stopping in the middle of the kitchen and looking absently at the stove, " if we could only have brought the church with us— and the graves, I would n't mind it. Or if only that mesa was moved back and I could see round the corner of it, it would n't be so bad.''

" Oh now, mother,'' said Anita, "just

quit thinking about it. We can drive you
up there sometimes on Sundays. Four
miles is n't but a step."

"It seems like a long step—like I was
in another world somehow. Anita, you
won't let Cornelio forget his promise, will
you ?"

"He won't forget. Besides, you 're
not going to be buried for a good many
years yet."

The little woman shook her head sadly.

"I do n't know," she said, "I do n't
know."

She would try to get out of these depressing moods, and went about busying
herself with Anita's work. And Anita,
who had a good enough heart but little
knowledge of the nature of her mother,
whistled from morning till night, with her
black hair hanging raggedly about her
brown face, and her dress, longer behind
than in front, spotted with the soot of the
kitchen. But her mother caught little of
the spirit of the whistling, and Anita found
her crying over the forks once, which she
held purposelessly in her wrinkled hands,
the knives lying neglected in the water.

And once the little woman forgot herself and dropped the teapot on the floor, and broke it and spilled its contents all about. She sank down and wept piteously, while Anita gathered up the pieces. The girl finally lifted her up and tried to comfort her.

"I'm just all gone, somehow," she said to Anita. "Oh, I just can't bear it. I've been there all my life,—and the three of them lying there day and night, and me not there. I never missed it once since they were put there—twice a day. They must notice it, Anita."

Some weeks went by, and the two children could not but see that the little woman was pining away. Her thin shoulders grew thinner still, and the very small form seemed visibly to shrink. The wrinkles on the face grew deeper and the pensive look increased. They would find her many times a day, and sometimes in the night when the moon shone and the prairies were still and bright, standing looking at the corner of the distant mesa. She was constantly in trouble over the promise of Cornelio, and made him very frequently repeat it.

She was sick a few days in the early summer, and in the fever talked only of Lauriano and José and Gertie. They feared it would be her end, but she grew better after a week, and was soon going about again. It was plain, however, that she was weaker. She was so frail that they half expected her to fall at any minute. And even the sturdy and thoughtless Cornelio felt an odd misgiving as he rode away in the morning, lest on his return at night he might find that she was dead.

Cornelio and Anita had a secret which they had kept from their mother till their hopes in it should be realized. They were in doubt as to the effect of it on the little woman. There came a day, however, when it must come out. Cornelio returned early in the evening and found his mother sitting by the kitchen fire pensively watching Anita. The girl was preparing the supper. Cornelio, watched by his sister, nervously poked the fire and fumbled with the battered kettle on the stove.

" Well, it 's come," he said presently to Anita. Anita stopped in her work.

"Mother, I 've got some good news," said Cornelio. The little woman turned her eyes absently to him.

"You 're always glad to hear I 'm getting on, are n't you, mother?"

"Why—why, yes, Cornelio; yes." She was a little startled; his manner was not easy.

"They 're going to make me sheriff, mother."

She looked about vaguely, seemed to consider it necessary to smile, but failed.

"It 's a good job and more money in it than this. It 's a mighty fine thing, mother."

Mrs. Serna looked helplessly at Anita, who tried to smile reassuringly.

"We 'll live in Springer, you know," went on Cornelio hurriedly; "a nice place there by the jail—fine place; you and Anita with me, you know."

The old woman's head went back against the chair.

"We 'll go in a few days," said Cornelio, desperately, "maybe to-morrow."

Mrs. Serna said nothing. She turned her head and looked out of the window at the distant mesa, then about upon the dishes and the floor. She seemed suddenly to think she must say something in agreement.

" It 's a—it 's a nice thing, Cornelio," she said.

After watching her a moment, Anita went on with the supper. In half an hour it was ready. Her mother was still sitting by the fire.

" How far is it?" said Mrs. Serna, at last.

" About twenty-five miles," replied Anita.

Mrs. Serna told them she could not eat any supper, and before it was dark she wanted Anita to put her to bed. They could see signs of the fever again, and before Anita left her for the night she was muttering occasionally to herself about Gertie and José and Lauriano.

The sun set at half-past six, and an hour later they found that Mrs. Serna was gone. They searched the house and the garden and the adobe stable, but she was not there. Her shawl, they found, was also gone. In consternation Cornelio and Anita stood and stared at one another.

" Saddle the horses, Cornelio, quick."

A little later they were on their way

toward the point of the mesa.   It was almost dark, and the trail was narrow and in
places rugged, but the horses were familiar
with it.   Neither of the riders had any
doubt as to the way she had gone.

Near the mesa, on a spot of rough and
stony ground, they found the shawl, its
worn fringe caught up into the scrub-oak
bush by the way.   In deep distress they
hurried on.   At last they could see the
old adobe house, now empty and forlorn;
and across the trail from it the deserted
chapel came dim out of the dusk.   When
they were fifty yards from the church,
they saw her staggering along in front of
them over the stones of the trail, close to
the door.   Bounding forward they beheld
her fall.   Coming now close to her, they
could see her crawling on the ground,
silently, stretching out her hands to the
door.   They reached it as soon as she,
but she sunk against the wood.

You can see her grave in there now, if
you go; only that the earthern floor is
flat above it as above the others, and they
must show you where it is.   But she is
beside José and Gertie and Lauriano.

HIS TERRIFYING NEMESIS

❦

YOU seen the cabin up yonder in the cañon, where the Blackwater Mesa trail comes down? I showed you, did n't I—where the rocks starts up on both sides? That's where Sue used to live. Lord, you ought to seen Sue. That woman was a terror to man an' beast. She was kind o' middle-sized, like, an' built heavy, a devil of a ways across the shoulders. First I knowed of her she come heavin' in from the south along with the slant-sidedest-mouthed boy you ever seen. The feller was n't more 'n twelve, an' white-headed an' screwed up in the face— Lord, the ungodliest-lookin' boy!

They was ridin' a couple o' rickety animals, with skillets an' bedtickin' an' guns an' one thing another tied onto a pore, little, measly burro. I seen 'em comin' up the trail, an' I could see the red o' that woman's face at two hunderd yards, an' the way her jaw was cut square-like.

She says her an' the boy, which she called Bill, was huntin' fer a cabin fer to stay in, havin' got part o' the Blackwater Mesa fer a little herd o' sheep that some cow-punchers was bringin' along up a mile er so behind, an' she heard I was n't usin' the one up the cañon, an' her an' Bill wanted it. I says, was there jus' her an' Bill? She says, Lord, she hoped so, an' turned around to the screw-faced young 'n', makin' him wince. I finally let 'em have it, an' before long they was settled.

They 'tended mostly to their own business, an' I would n't 'a' knowed they was there 'cept sometimes of a still evenin' I could hear Bill whistlin' 'way up yonder, er maybe yellin' at bein' beat. An' sometimes she 'd come down to borrow somethin' er ask about one thing another.

After while, though, it was different. The days goin' on, she used to be here most ever' evenin', sometimes leavin' Bill locked up. You could hear him hollerin'. An' she 'd set in here an' talk about bein' lonesome. There was n't nobody here

then but me an' Ofelia, old Mexican cook
I used to keep, an' a cow-puncher. An'
she 'd set fer hours talkin' about how lonesome she was, an' the sheep, an' rheumatism, an' one thing another. She says
how hard it was fer a woman with instincks fer to be an old maid. She laid a
heap o' store by her instincks, an' 'lowed
in a harsh sort o' voice that things around
did n't suit her somehow.

It was n't till she had done like that several times that I begun to see she had her
eyes on me. Lord, the joke tickled me.
So I humored her, an' told her candid that
she did n't have no sentiment. I says a
woman ought to be kind o' gentle like an'
soft, which she could see herself she lacked
a sight o' bein'. I says to camm down' an'
kind o' soften up. She was mighty free
an' open, but so hard like an' straight-
for'ard.

Well, I was in Watrous one day, an' a
feller come up to me an' says he was from
Missouri. He was the measliest-lookin'
man I ever seen, 'bout twenty-six years
old, an' short an' kind o' crushed up in the
face. He had stringy white hair an' a little

fuzz o' mustache white an' greased. He was kind o' dressed-up-lookin', only out of a pore kind o' store clo'es. I'm a perty tough old hoss an' lived out wild a most devilish long while, but I can tell a man what is dressed up from a man what ain't got sense enough to know that he ain't.

This feller says he was here fer his health an' wanted to git out where it was wild. He says he'd pay a good price fer board, if I'd let him come. I was needin' the money, an' I finally done it.

First night he was here Sue come down, an' Bill follerin'. Bill he stayed out in the kitchen eatin', an' Sue come in an' set down. She got up a talk with the feller from Missouri, an' I could see her eyein' him close all evenin'. I might as well call him Siss at the start, fer that's what all us cow-punchers got to callin' him. His name was somethin' like Crisistus, but the cowboys got turned against him an' says he was a no-'count cuss, anyhow.

Well, Sue talked a heap about its bein' lonesome fer a female out here, an' wanted to know all about Missouri, an' come mighty near wearin' the little cuss out.

An' when she went home I could see by
the way she saddled up her horse an' cussed
Bill that somethin' new was comin' in
sight. An' after her an' Bill had pulled
out, Siss he set kind o' subdued-like an'
did n't say much.

After that she come regular an' in-
vited him up there, but he would n't never
go. He always looked all kind o' done
up. Lord, she was twice as big as him.
An' her an' Bill 'd stay fer dinner er supper, an' she 'd set opposite Siss an' eat like
it was a steady business with her. But
Bill he was the eatinest boy ever I seen.
That white-headed, screw-face young 'n'
'd chew so devilish elaborate that Siss 'd
lay down his knife an' fork an' not eat
nothin'.

After while I could see him watchin'
fer her ever' day out o' the winder. An'
when he 'd see her comin' he 'd light out.
But she 'd set around till he come back.
An' sometimes she 'd come in on him
without him expectin' it, an', Lord, he 'd
jus' look plumb miserble. I knowed he
dreaded the sight of her, an' yet, d' you
know, I had an idea there was somethin'

kind o' fascinatin' about it. I 've seen him git pale an' shake, hearin' her comin' around the house, an' yet he 'd set right up by the hour, spite of himself, an' mumble along, her forcin' him into it.

It went on like that fer a good many weeks, an' I could see Sue was gittin' discouraged, but she did n't let up. Once when he was gone she come in an' set there where you 're settin' an' looked sorry. She went on as to how deep her feelin' fer him was, how it jus' come up sudden an' overwhelmin', an' what was she to do? I says I thought already she was doin' ever'thing a lady could reasonable be expected to do. But she says she appeared to be makin' mighty pore headway, fer he was cold, somehow—not touched none.

I says: "Sue, it 's like this, what I told you before—you ain't got no sentiment."

She says somehow she could n't git the hang of it.

I says: "You want to be soft-like — not so turrible. It 's fer a woman to be gentle."

"Well," she says, kind o' hard, "ain't I gentle? Lord, Si, I 've done a sight o'

holdin' in on his account. You ought to
see what I can be."

"But Sue," I says, "the trouble is jus'
this. You ain't female enough."

She took it sorrowful, an' leaned over
an' thought some, an' says:

"Lord, I'd be more if I knowed how.
I'm jus' goin' along natural, an' I can't
help its not bein' no softer. Somehow it
do n't feel soft. Cussed if I believe it is
soft. I never was no hand at what you
call sentiment. I do n't know what it
means, much, unless it's like chuckin'
him under the chin an' one thing another.
I reckon I could do that with practice, but
it'd come unhandy, somehow, an' besides
I believe it'd scare him."

"Lord," I says, "it would, Sue; there
ain't no doubt of it. But there ain't no
use goin' to extremes. Now chuckin'
him under the chin at this stage o' the
game," I says, "would be goin' to extremes. Come it lighter, more gradual."
I looked solemn at her, an' pointed with
my finger at her like this, an' I says:

"I'll tell you what, Sue, with a woman
it's mostly the eyes. Them's the things

that counts. You want to practice 'em up. Git 'em by all odds to lookin' languider. Languid is the word. With a energetic critter like you, Sue, it 'll be mighty difficult, I know, fer you do n't feel languid, not by a devil of a sight; but practice 'em up."

She set up straight, makin' them shoulders o' hers look twice as broad. She says:

"Would that do it ? "

I says : "If it was done thorough, it would do it."

She says she could n't think o' nothin' that 'd come harder. She says she 'd rather break a even dozen bronchos any day. But she reckoned the thing 'd have to be done.

I says : "It ain't so hard if you can git the hang of it. It comes mostly from lookin' sideways 'stead o' straight." I says : "Notice all them women that 's well-married, an' nine out o' ten of 'em looks sideways, kind o' tender-like, er if they do n't it 's because they 've got out of the habit of it." I says : "You do n't appear to do nothin' delicate enough. Sue, you 've got to work yourself up tenderer."

She was lookin' all beat out. She says she guessed it was the last hope, but, Lord, she dreaded it.

·I says : " It ain't only the last hope, Sue. You ought n't to begin lookin' at it morbid that way. That's unhealthy. It's a female privilege, that's what it is—a female privilege. It ought to give you a meller feelin'. Why, Sue," I says, " ain't you got nothin' in no ways *sweet* in you ? "

She shook her head kind o' sad an' says she had never laid no store by any sich things. She says : " Sich things, Si, I know 'd be mighty unpleasant an' troublesome to have. It'd be like eatin' too much. But if it 's necessary, I wished to the Lord I had 'em, an' in any quantity so 's they 'd do the work ; an' I 'd be willin' to stand it. An' what 's more, Si, I 'm ready now to begin workin' 'em up. I 'll try fer all I 'm worth, by thunder, to be delicate-like an' languider ! "

Well, she done it. An', Lord, it was pitiful. The days goin' by, the effect on Siss was worse. He got so he could n't run, ner have no energy to hide, ner nothin'. When he 'd hear her comin' he 'd jus' git pale an' kind o' shrivel all up, an' set down silent an' wait fer her to come in. I never seen a man so turrible fascinated, an' dreadin' the very air, too, all the time, fer fear she was somewheres in it. It jus' eat the health right out o' the pore little cuss.

All along while she was tryin' to be tender, she got even with herself on Bill. It was turrible the spite she took out on that screw-faced young 'n'. It done her good, when Siss was n't nowheres near, to cuss Bill an' club him around. An' she told me private that the only way she could work herself up in any ways tender was to whale Bill before she come down, an' I guess she done it. An' Bill he hated Siss like poison, fer he seen how it was; an' ever' time he seen him he ducked his head an' went off mutterin'. An' Siss, somehow he got thinner. I could see the thing was workin' unhealthy on his mind, an' he growed morbid-like.

I seen it was workin' up to a point, fer neither of 'em could stand it much longer without somethin' happenin'. Fer a day er two Sue was discouraged again. I could tell it by the way she let Bill alone an' did n't cuss him er nothin'. After while she come to me.

"Si," she says "I 'm afraid it ain't doin' no good."

I says: "You 've got him overcome. He do n't say nothin', because it 's too strong on him."

She says: "I think, by the Lord, it 's my duty to say it out plain, then, if he do n't."

I wanted to see the thing come to some kind of a head, an' I agreed. I says: "Well, I reckon you 're right—only do it meller."

I think Bill got the ungodliest beatin' that night that he ever seen, an' the next mornin' I was in the stable there where the dobeys is out, leavin' that hole at the back. They thought I was down the medder, an' she found him settin' on an old piece of a hay-rake back there where I could see through the hole, they bein' outside an' me inside. She says kind o' holler:

"Ain't I tender enough?"

Siss, he shrunk up an' did n't say nothin'.

She says: "'Cause it's pure female affection, whatever it looks like."

Siss, he begun to shake some.

She says: "I never had the hang o' bein' delicate an' fondlin', an' maybe that's why you ain't seen through it. But, Lord, I've done a devil of a sight o' cuitivatin' it!"

Siss was jus' plumb white. She went on an' says:

"This has been the wearinest thing that ever come on me. I recognize that I did n't know how to handle it, an' it's nigh made me crazy. But it's real stuff, an' I want you to take it like it is. I've done all I knowed how to put somethin' soft in it. I'm made kind o' different, somehow, an' it come hard, but if it 'il work I'm glad I done it. Say, was there anything wrong with it?"

Siss, he was in a cold sweat, settin' still as a corpse, an lookin' at her 'bout half way up. She waited a minute an' says:

"O Lord! do n't take no account o' what it looks like. What it is, is *love*. I've done said it now. It's a word that comes hard an' do n't seem to fit nothin',

but that's what it is. I never knowed
how to make it look like that, an' was
afraid you could n't see it. I knowed
myself I did n't have the hang of it, an'
cussed myself fer makin' it look like
ever'thing else but that. I knowed all
along it was failin' fer its looks. That's
why I 've said it out plain. Do n't you
believe that 's what it is ? "

It was pitiful to see Siss, an' Sue shifted
back'ards an' for'ards an' begun again. She
says :

" Honest, I 've done ever'thing I
knowed how. What else can I do now but
jus' plain *say* what it is ? An' ain't I done
said it ? It sounds out o' shape, but I
done it the best I knowed how, an' if I
had any idea it was necessary I 'd do it
again, though it ain't natural. I hope to
the Lord you understand it out clear an'
full, fer I 'll tell you what it is, I can't
stand the unnatural strain o' this much
more. Say, is it all right ? "

Siss kind o' groaned. Sue, she looked
on beat out, an' finally she set her jaw an'
out with it.

" Well, by thunder ! " she says, loud,

" it 's this !   I want to marry you.   Say, it 's wearin' me out, an' I 'll say the whole thing clean to the limit.   Will you marry me ? "

She stood over him an' stared at him, fergittin' all about tryin' to be tender. An', by thunder, the thing worked! How she ever done it I do n't see.   She must 'a' had him tangled in the head, somehow, fer after a minute o' starin' at her he jus' throwed up his hands an' says, kind o' wild :

" O, Lord, Lord, yes ! "

Then she slid down an' did n't say no more.

Sue, she heard that the priest from Vegas was to be up at Rayado in two weeks, an' that evenin' she had it all laid out that Siss an' her was to borrow my wagon an' take one o' her horses an' one o' mine, her other one bein' lame, an' go up there then an' git the thing done.   An' the time goin' on, all them two weeks Siss looked jus' plumb miserble. Sue, she dropped all her soft ways o' puttin' on, right off.   She come to me, though, soon after she had fixed it up, an' says she owed

me a heap fer showin' her how, that I'd
'a' been surprised to see how smooth it
worked, an' that as long as she lived she'd
never cease to thank the Lord me an' her
got together an' figgered it out.

Well, it went on like that till about
three days before the day the priest was
comin' to Rayado, Siss lookin' miserbler
an' miserbler, an' her nailin' things here
an' there around the house, an' one thing
another, an' sailin' round after him. 'Long
about that time, one evenin' there was a
brother of Ofelia's, old Mexican from up
round Raton, come an' told Ofelia that he
was in a heap o' trouble about a girl o'
his what wanted to run off with a feller
him an' her ma hated. He had took the
girl to Springer an' left her there with
another brother o' theirs, an' come out
here to see if he could n't bring her out.
He says he wanted to git her away off
from anywheres, like this, an' keep her
here fer a while an' see if she would n't
git over it. I did n't raise no objection,
an' the next day about noon he come an'
left her here.

She was a slim sort o' girl, 'long about

nineteen, an' kind o' smart an' sassy-
lookin'. I seen that sassy way she had
o' jerkin' her head, quick as she got out
o' the wagon. An', Lord, but her eyes
was black! She was n't by no means a
bad-lookin' girl; do n't know but I 'd call
her uncommon perty, if it had n't been fer
somethin' kind o' wild-lookin' an' mussed-
up about her.

Well, I begun to see trouble before she 'd
been in the house an hour. I could
see it in the way Siss eyed at her. Why,
that feller had n't hardly looked up off the
floor fer two weeks. She made herself at
home, an' jus' took the whole house in
without no delay; an' I seen Siss's eyes
follerin' her around from one place to another, an' his hands twitchin' like. An'
he went around the rest o' the evenin' in a
sort o' dream.

Sue come down, too, an' Bill follerin'.
An' Sue seen somethin' in him immediate
that scented o' trouble, an' she watched
the girl an' cussed Bill a heap. The girl's
name was Josefita, an' I seen, too, that the
thing was mighty comical to her. She

watched them two like she 'd give a devil
of a sight to git some fun out of 'em.

Well, next mornin' I heard her git up
spry an' whistlin', an' I seen in her eyes
that somethin' was up. She had a kind o'
glitter in 'em, an' went around laughin' an'
havin' a devil of a time. An' along about
breakfast she begun to work it. She begun
lookin' sweet an' interested at Siss, an' no-
ticin' him plain, an' at breakfast she set next
him an' done a heap to draw him out.
She 'd smile—Lord! an' throw her sassy
head around an' look at Siss sideways, an'
jus' run on mixin' up talk an' laugh an'
smilin' an' one thing another. An' before
the meal was over Siss hove a big sigh, an'
laid down his fork, an' did n't eat no more.
You see, she had all them things Sue had
tried to put on, an' had 'em uncommon
too; an' it was sich a change to Siss that I
reckon he felt like a famishin' man that 's
found water. It was curious to watch
him. That was the day before the one
Sue had set to go to Rayado an' git married.

I was watchin' Josefita an' anticipatin'

somethin' all along, an' thought a heap all
day about had n't I ought to step in an'
keep her down. I done jus' one thing
wrong. I waited too long. But, Lord,
it 's natural enough she fooled me too.
That woman could 'a' fooled the angel
Gabriel. If she 'd set them eyes on him
an' begin workin' it up sweet, cussed if he
would n't leave his horn an' foller her
off.

The way she done it I did n't learn fer
a long while, but accordin' to what she
told afterward it was like this. She had
him plumb crazy by noon. Along after
dinner she roped him in to walkin' down
the medder with her, an' around that little
mesa yonder, while Sue was up to her
house gittin' the last things ready—an'
Bill. Then I reckon she gethered herself
up an' begun.

She told me afterward she begun pitiful
about bein' kep' off here, away from anybody that sympathized with her er knowed
how deep her feelin's was. Well, that
kind o' set Siss's insides to flutterin' around.
Finally he says out strong that he could
sympathize with her; he knowed how it

was. She says she was endurin' it all alone, an' it made her heart feel like it would bust. Siss, he said he pitied her from the bottom o' his, an' he wished to the Lord he was so fixed he could do somethin'.

Then Josefita turned round an' looked clean through him ungodly sweet, an' jus' carried him off his feet. She said she knowed it was unwomanlike to talk to a stranger this way, an' she felt she had n't the right to, an' her conscience hurt her, but her bosom was so full she jus' could n't help it, a woman's feelin's bein' unable to keep in after a certain point; an' anybody could see right off that he was a true kind of a man with a big heart. An' she asked him if he had less respect fer her fer doin' it.

An' Siss, he come out an' says, fer the Lord no! she showed herself to be in ever' particular a woman he admired, an' fer her to jus' talk right out—it done him good.

Josefita, she walked on silent a while to let it work in. An' perty soon she turned an' looked at him like that way again that jus' took his breath, an' says, since she had got to know him better an' feel that

he was a man she could trust an' look up
to as a friend, she naturally did n't want
to do nothin' to hurt his idea of her; an'
she was afraid he misunderstood her.

Siss, he swore up an' down he did n't
understand nothin' bad of her, an' if he
had, why, Lord, jus' her looks was enough.

But Josefita, she says she knowed she
had been represented as wild after another
feller in Raton, an' she could n't bear not
to tell Siss the whole truth; she 'd feel
like violatin' the trust he put in her. So
she 'd confess that at first she had liked
that feller. She says how sorrowful it was
that a young girl did n't always know her
own heart, an' sometimes let it lead her
away. She drawed in her breath an'
turned around at Siss again an' says, of
late, jus' since she come here, the pure air
an' the mountains, an' in particular the
kind folks around an' the feelin' o' sym-
pathy, had showed her how she had went
astray, an' made her see herself better.
An' she says she hoped he would n't think
no less of her fer bein' so foolish.

Well, I guess Siss was jus' overcome,
an' talked wild about what a heap more he

admired her fer it, an' how it showed that
her nature was lovin' an' tender, a thing a
woman had ought to be. He says, lookin'
up toward the cañon where Sue lived, that
if there was one thing in the world his
nature yearned fer it was some kind o'
tender feelin' like hers.

Josefita says what she admired in a man,
maybe even more than lots o' feelin', was
a big, darin' nature. She says she could
see, now that her eyes was opened, that
the feller in Raton was n't free an' darin'
enough. She says she could love a man
that could wade through a devil of a sight
fer her, an' do uncommon sudden things
if necessary. Them was the things to be
most admired in a man. An' she looked
at Siss again, an' says did n't he think so?

Siss was sweatin' a little, thinkin' about
Sue, but he come out bold an' says he sure
did, an' a man that would n't was n't
worth havin' her. She says, lookin' at him
deep-like, that a man like that could have
her undyin' love, an' she 'd cling to him
through the worst that could be got up.

I reckon that done the work; an' Siss
jus' poured it out. He begun an' he told

her ever'thing, an' says how it was that
Sue had jus' shut the sun out o' the sky, an'
took all the snap out of him, an' made
him clean crazy, so that he had n't knowed
what he was doin' when he got himself
into it. He says he had passed through
weeks o' misery like nobody ever dreamed
of before, that his nights was nightmares
an' his days swamps, that he had n't
looked fer no hope till Josefita come. He
says she was like the promised land to
him, an' already he worshiped her perfectly mad. He says as fer darin', why,
his love fer her had all the darin' o' terror;
an' Lord, could n't they manage somehow
to git out o' this!

Josefita was jus' clean surprised at its
workin' so well, but she kep' her head an'
give in slow, an' finally it was fixed up.
You see that was her scheme from the
first, to git away. She knowed she
could n't do it by herself.

Sue had been cuttin' round at a devil of
a rate all day, gittin' things fixed up fer
the day follerin', makin' a new step at the
door, an' fixin' up the harness, an' greas-
in' the wagon, an' one thing another.

An' Bill, he crawled round holdin' nails an' fetchin' hammers an' things, an' gittin' cussed at. Since the thing had been fixed up, Bill had n't had no easier time. Sue 'd whale him jus' because she felt high-strung. Ever' time she 'd see Siss she 'd feel so worked up at its havin' come out all right, that she 'd take it out on Bill. An', Lord, how Bill hated the whole thing! He laid all his trouble on Siss; an' it was that that come into play with Josefita. Nothin' got away from that woman. She figgered it out like this.

In the first place the thing had to be done that night, fer jus' let mornin' come an' Sue come sailin' round, an' she knowed it 'd all be up with Siss. It was goin' to be a dark night, an' they had to go up the west trail towards the mountains, fer the other goes down the prairie towards Springer, where they might meet somebody that knowed 'em. The Cimarron trail, towards the mountains, is mighty rough, an' unless you 're a good driver an' know it like a book, why drivin' it in the dark is jus' plumb impossible, an' she knowed it.

So she figgered it out that they'd git
the wagon an' the horses ready at the first
sign o' daylight. Lord, Sue had 'em all
fixed an' ready the night before, right here
at the shed. Then they was to pull out,
him an' her, the minute there was any
light at all. She knowed there was n't
no dependence to be put on Sue's bein'
asleep, an' she was afraid Sue'd run onto
'em startin', er, anyhow, hear the wagon,
fer the trail up that way do n't run no
great ways from the cañon.

Well, she finally got Bill off behind the
shed. She worked on his hatin' Siss an'
stretched it, an' says Bill was right, that it
sure was Siss that made Sue beat him.
She says as long as Siss stayed, there
was n't no use o' Bill expectin' no peace.
Bill says he knowed it. So she told him
plain that her an' Siss was goin' to run
off, an' asked him if he did n't wish they
would; an' the screw-faced young 'n' says,
Lord, yes, he'd do anything he knowed
how to help 'em.

So she says, did he reckon he could begin along about one er two o'clock in the
night to gittin' sick, so 's Sue 'd be occu-

pied tendin' to him. Bill says he could git sick, but, Lord, no ordinary sick o' his 'd bother Sue none. Josefita says, well, could n't he work up somethin' that would bother her.

Bill, he thought, an' screwed up his face an' scratched that there white head o' his, an' after while says he could have a fit. He says if he jus' had it ordinary it would n't make no difference to Sue, but he 'd make it so tremendous uncommon that she could n't help herself. He says he 'd have it in the middle o' them clo'es she had laid out fer the weddin', an' that 'd fetch her. Josefita was took back at the size of it, but she seen it was a fine thing. Only, she says, was he sure he could handle it long enough? Bill says, let him alone fer that. So they fixed it up.

The last thing Sue done was to come sailin' down an' tell Siss she 'd be up by first daybreak, an' she wanted him to be ready. She eyed Josefita a heap, but Lord, Josefita was as sweet an' innocent as you ever seen, an' finally Sue went off up the path to the cañon fer the night, an' Bill follerin'.

I reckon Bill did n't sleep none that night. I think he must 'a' set up in the dark waitin', an' along a little before the first break o' day he set up the ungodliest racket an' breakin' things that the Lord ever let run on. I seen the house afterwards, an' there was the marks of it ever'-wheres. But he must 'a miscalculated er got wore out er somethin', fer he finally let up an' expected her to light in an' beat him, which 'd occupy her a heap; but she never done it. She set down an' lit in to mendin' them clo'es up desperate', an' fixin' things so 's they 'd do. I reckon it was about then that she heard the rattle o' the wagon.

About daybreak I thought in the middle of a dream, like a feller will, that I heard a noise outside, an' directly I woke up an' was listenin' to the wheels goin' off up the trail. Sounded like my wagon. By the time I got dressed an' went out, they was 'way up yonder past where the path to the cañon joins the trail. I was jus' a-wonderin' what kind of a earthquake Sue 'd turn loose, when I seen her runnin' out o'

the cañon after 'em at a turrible gait, with
a lasso in her hand, swingin' it around her
head.

Josefita had the lines, an' she seen her
when she got perty nigh up, dodgin'
around a little bunch o' scrub-oak that's
up that way, an' Lord, maybe she did n't
lay whip to them horses ! Siss he hung
onto the seat, an' they lit out on a gallop.
If that little black-eyed Spanish woman
had 'a' been a second later with her whip,
it 'd been all up with Siss, fer the rope
did n't miss him a foot. It caught the
brake an' pulled out o' Sue's hand, an' the
wagon went tearin' on with Josefita layin'
on with the whip an' lookin' back kind o'
wild an' sassy, an' Siss holdin' on as white
as a sheet. Sue she stood in the trail, an'
when I come up she jus' looked stunned,
an' it was a long time before I could git
her away.

Well, the thing was done, an' they was
gone, an' there was n't no help fer it, fer
there was n't but one other horse here then
besides that lame one o' hers', an' I had the
rheumatism an' would n't 'a' mixed in the

thing, noways. I knowed I 'd git the wagon back somehow. Think of her working it up in forty-eight hours!

Fer two days Bill ner Sue did n't come down, an' it was gloomy round here with Ofelia whimperin' about the girl's bein' gone. Then along one evenin' Sue come walkin' down, kind o' subdued, Bill foller-in'. She come in an' set there fer a long time. Finally she says she was soured. She looked like it too. I tried to think o' somethin' to say, but Lord, there jus' was n't nothin', an' I set still. After while she broke out hard-like at me, an' says she believed I showed her how wrong. She says sentiment was kind o' like fever, that was n't no natural way o' warmin' up, but jus' burnt out. I jus' smoked an' did n't say nothin'.

After while she said she guessed gener-ally, when people turned soured, they wanted to git away from the world an' stay where it 's lonesome an' never see nobody. She says it was n't that way with her. She says it made her restless. She says mornin' was jus' as miserble as night to her, an' night jus' as miserble as mornin', an' she 'd been ponderin' a heap about goin' off somewheres.

"Sue," I says, "what you want is somethin' to take your mind off it."

She says it was soured on it, but somethin' might make it a heap lighter. She says she seen that little cuss in a dream ever' night, an' woke up swearin' at him in her sleep.

I says: "I 'll tell you what you do, Sue. Why do n't you go to Springer an' run a hotel?"

She looked up steady an' thought a heap.

I says: "They ain't but one hotel there, an' it 's high-priceder than us rangers likes when we go to town. You could run it specially fer rangers, an' like as not ketch enough trade to git along. Bill, he could help around a heap."

She set fer mighty near an hour thinkin' about it, an' finally she says:

"Si, I 'll do it."

After talkin' about it some, she says:

"It 'll keep my mind off bein' soured on ever'thing. Maybe I 'll fergit them cussed two an' quit seein' 'em at night.

An' there's one thing, Si," she says, gittin' up solemn an' lookin' at me hard an' firm, "I'm done, now an' forevermore, with bein' in any ways soft. Never, long as I live, so help me the Lord, will I fool no more with sentiment. By thunder, I'm female enough!"

With that she went out, an' Bill follerin'. An' in two weeks she was gone to Springer an' set up a little one-hoss hotel what she called the Rangers' Paradise. An' it was n't more 'n a couple o' weeks more till a Mexican come bringin' back the wagon. He says a little white-headed feller an' a Spanish-lookin' woman had give him money to fetch it back. He did n't know only that they was over at a little station on the narrow-gauge the other side o' the mountains, an' says they had borrowed the wagon an' did n't need it no more.

It was 'long towards round-up time, an' I heard somethin' about new freight-rates on the railroad fer cattle, an' went to Springer one day to do a little tradin' an' find out. I et dinner at Sue's an' talked to her some. She had Bill with an apern makin' him wait on the table. She says she was gittin' some over it, but time only showed that she was really turned soured.

'Long towards four o'clock I heard there was a cattle-buyer over at the old hotel, an' went an' hunted him up. I made a deal with him, an' was still settin' in what they called the parlor, figgerin' out how much the cattle was comin' to, the cattle-buyer havin' gone.

Perty soon I heard the door open behind me. I turned around an' seen Josefita standin' there lookin' at me that sassy way o' hers. She set down cool an' talked an' acted like she 'd been settin' there camm ever since she was born; an' finally I got the whole thing out of her.

She told me a long tale about how she hauled Siss around down to Santa Fé by the narrow-gauge, an' to Las Vegas, an' one place another, an' finally his money had give out jus' as they got here. She says she had promised him all along to marry him soon as they got to Raton, an' she had fixed herself up with her folks. But, Lord, she did n't want me to think she meant it. She says all along she wanted to jus' git to Springer an' git money from her uncle an' pull out an' leave Siss an' go home an' behave herself. She says now she had got here her uncle would n't let her have the money, an' I was her last hope. Would n't I please lend her jus' car-fare to Raton? I says, where was Siss? an' she says he was down at the stores somewheres.

Well, I thought a devil of a sight, an' finally I done it. I thought, after all, it was the best thing there was. She says all she wanted was to git full rid o' Siss, an' Lord help her if she ever tried to run away with another man. It looked kind o' tough on Siss, but I never did like the little cuss nohow, an' he might as well learn things all of a sudden as drag 'em out slow.

Then she asked all about Sue, kind o' interested. I says Sue was in town an' keepin' another hotel around the corner. Lord, you ought to seen her eyes open! After she had took the idea full in, I begun to see the devil comin' back in her. Her eyes begun to dance, an' perty soon she bust out an' laughed. Then she jumped up quick an' says:

" I 'm goin' to do it! "

" Do what? " I says.

" I 'm goin' to send him to Sue's hotel! "

I jus' leaned back nigh speechless an' says, " O Lord! "

" It 's me that took him away," she says, " an' it 's me that 'll bring him back! "

I tried to git her not to, but it was n't no use. You could n't persuade her out o' nothin' she had her head set on. So perty soon she got up an' left, an' I went out on the street in a little while myself.

I seen a good many cowboys that was acquainted out this way standin' around in bunches with their horses, talkin', an' I come to find out that some of 'em had jus' seen Siss was in town, an' was meditatin' doin' somethin' to him. They all hated Siss an' stuck up fer Sue. I told 'em I believed he was goin' to Sue's hotel by mistake. They seen trouble right away, an' started round fer Sue's place to see it an' help her out if she needed 'em.

Josefita had went steppin' down the street an' hunted up Siss at a little old store out o' the way, fer Siss did n't like the idea o' showin' himself. She says to him that her uncle 'd give her the money in the mornin', so they 'd have to stay in Springer over night. She says it would n't be in no ways wise fer 'em to be at the same hotel, an' there was a mighty nice new hotel over here jus' started up. Siss, he done ever'-thing she said, so he went to Sue's.

Me an' the cowboys was comin' round the corner by Sue's, when we heard her shriekin' inside, an' next minute here come Siss tearin' out o' the hotel without no hat. I never seen sich a livin' picture o' terror. He made a kind o' low, sandy-colored streak round into the next street, an' Sue come bustin' out clean gone crazy; an' Bill follerin'. She stood on the step, red an' pantin' an' yellin':

"Ketch him! Ketch him! Fer the Lord ketch him. O Lord! O Lord!"

Ever' cowboy there stuck spurs in his horse an' set out at a run after Siss, gittin' their ropes ready as they went. I reckon they chased him about a half-mile up the railroad track, an' up yonder where the cattle-pens is two of 'em that was ahead lassoed him. So here, perty soon, they come bringin' him back, leadin' him.

When they got to that open place there between the old hotel an' the depot, here Sue come, trottin' kind o' heavy, with her sleeves rolled up, showin' them turrible arms o' hers, an' a big cattle-whip in her hand, an' Bill follerin'. She was hollerin' kind o' hoarse :

" Let me at him! Hold him there, now ! Jus' hold him ! O Lord !"

About six o' them cow-punchers lassoed Siss an' stood their horses with the other ends o' the ropes out in a circle around him, holdin' him drawed up tight in the middle; an' most ever'body in town was watchin'. Siss's knees was shakin' turrible, an' I tried to stop 'em from doin' it, but it was n't no use. An' Sue, she come in between two o' the ropes, an' she planted her feet hard, an' she jus' lit in an' give that feller the ungodliest beatin' that I ever seen a human bein' git. An' Bill set on a pile o' cross-ties an' watched, drinkin' it in. An' in the middle of it I looked up, an' seen Josefita at the hotel winder. She looked at me like she was sorry she done it.

When Sue was plumb wore out, she let

up an' went off up to the hotel, all tired
down an' slow, draggin' the whip, an' her
sleeves still rolled up; an' Bill follerin'.
They turned Siss loose, an' the last I ever
seen o' that feller was next mornin' ridin'
off towards Texas on a miserble old
horse somebody took pity on him an' give
him.

I give the money to Josefita, an' she
kep' quiet at the hotel, so Sue never seen
her, an' went off up to Raton that night.
An' when I went an' seen Sue, she says
she guessed she was satisfied, an' things
had worked out better 'n she ever expected,
an' she thought her an' Bill 'd do better
with the hotel now it was off her mind.
An' Bill, he went round whistlin'.

COLD FACTS AT THE TAVERN

❦

AT nightfall two cowboys rode up to the "tavern" under the mesa, picketed their horses across the trail, and entered the bar-room. They were lean, smooth-faced fellows, one of them light of complexion and boisterous of manner, the other darker, shorter, and the possessor of a quizzical expression of countenance. Beside the smirking bar-keeper no one else was in the room but a man of much whisker, who sat in a corner with his hat jammed down over his eyes.

"Rattle 'em up, rattle 'em up, Scaps!" said he of the boisterous manner, who answered to the name of Mac. "Me and Bill's thirsty—rattle 'em up!"

Scaps accordingly rattled them up to the extent of two foaming glasses. There was a round table in the middle of the room, and the two took chairs beside it.

" Will Petie be along ? " queried Mac. " Why, bless my soul—" suddenly breaking off, " if it ain't Jimmie ! " He arose hilariously and clapped him of the whiskers resoundingly on the back. " Jimmie, old boy ! Ha, ha ! The Lord help us, Bill, if it ain't Jimmie ! "

Jimmie appeared somewhat disconcerted. He lifted his hat and did an honorary smile of recognition. But the surroundings in general seemed to interest him not much.

" Cussed if it ain't," said Bill, getting up and eyeing the man with much interest.

" Well, it 's me — yes ; and there 's an end of it. Who 's Petie ? "

" Petie 's a cow-puncher, or a bum, or something. He 's more fun than a hoss-race. Ha, ha ! You ought to hear Petie tell a yarn, now. You 'd laugh yourself sick. Rattle 'em up, Scaps, rattle 'em up ! "

" Is he comin' ? " inquired Bill.

" Sure," said Scaps.

Indeed, at that moment Petie himself appeared, coming in at the door, whistling gently to himself and looking about. He

was a small, slight man, somewhat seedy
in appearance, with a slouch hat, sharp
eyes, a comical expression, little round
face, and fat cheeks like those of a baby.
But it must have been a dissipated baby to
wear so reddish-pink a complexion. Petie
clasped his chin with his fingers, made a
grimace at the assembly, and whistled to
himself. Then he said, absently :

" Mac, Bill, and Whiskers—regular set
o' devils."

The remark called forth uproarious
laughter from the first, a critical smile
from the second, and a grunt of disgust
from the third of the gentlemen named.

" Rattle 'em up for the crowd," said
Petie, taking his seat on a high stool by
the bar, with his thumbs in his vest and
his back to the bartender.

" Well, light in for a yarn," said Bill,
settling his feet farther under the table.

" Which ? " said Petie, inquiringly.

" Tell us a story — tell us a story,"
said Mac. " Thunder, what are you here
for ? "

" Brother Whiskers," said Petie, pointing with his thumb, " might be annoyed."

" Aw, let up," growled the voice under the whiskers; " go on—go on. It ain't nothin' to me! "

Petie smiled an odd smile.

" If I told you this here tale, gentlemen, you 'd say it was a lie."

The hilarious Mac deemed this a sufficiently ludicrous introduction. Bill smiled deprecatingly.

" O no, O no," he observed.

Petie twisted his feet into the rounds of the stool and looked about again shrewdly at the company.

" Hard lines to be called a liar; but, boys, I 've got to risk it. It 's weighin' on my mind. This here tale is as true as the Catholic Church, by San Francisco! "

" Go on, go on! "

" You know how the grass grows — Looky here, Bill; you 're too critical; do n't eye a feller like that; it ain't right. Well, you know how the grass grows around here."

" We know how it do n't grow," said Bill.

" Well, then, you know how it do n't

grow. There 's spots where it do grow, and spots where it do n't grow. She sticks up in bunches; she do n't grow all together, thick, like a front yard."

"Psh!" said he of the whiskers, suddenly lowering himself in his chair in an expression of disgust.

Petie eyed the interrupter with a great and bright smile playing over his features.

"She grows several inches apart," continued Petie.

"Ha, ha!" broke in he of the hilarious manner, in sudden and causeless mirth.

"Well, gentlemen," said Petie, in some concern, "do n't go and see points to the tale before it 's got any. Why, thunder, I ain't begun!"

"Well, hurry up!" put in Bill. "You ain't artistic."

"She grows several inches apart, and when it 's dry she dies out some and gits farther apart, so that it 's bare land in between. And when it gits dryer she gits still farther apart, and it 's a foot or so from one bunch to the other."

"Well, it ain't," said Jimmie; "it all dies down alike." His tone was one of unutterable scorn. Petie merely smiled the bright smile.

"When I was young," he said, "it did n't rain for a remarkable long time. We set around prayin' for it, and the cattle come up and stood around, and we was prayin' and the cattle was bawlin', and altogether we raised a deuce of a row; but it did n't rain. Well, these here bunches of grass got thinner and thinner. At the start there was five or six inches between 'em; first we knowed there was a foot. It was the same way all over New Mexico and Colorado and Arizona, and Lord knows where all. 'Long in July it was as dry—O, well, as dry as Jimmie! Rattle 'em up, Scaps!"

Jimmie failed to repress his grunt of contempt.

"You 're spreadin' it out too much," said the critical Bill; "you ain't artistic."

"Dryer 'n Jimmie," mused Mac, shaking his head in profound amusement. "Well, what happened then?"

"Why, along in August and September and October we kept on prayin' for rain, and the cattle got thinner and the grass growed farther apart. Ordinary times a steer gits enough to eat just walkin' about, natural, but when the grass got so far apart, that way would n't work."

"Why, how did they git enough?" queried Bill.

"By trottin'."

"Which?"

"Sure thing. Trottin'. Nippin' the bunches on the trot. Seen 'em do it many a time. They could gather up enough that way. Them as could n't trot from one bunch to the other, died."

He of the whiskers turned his back to the others, thrust his feet against the wall, and pulled his hat down farther over his eyes. The liquor which the gentleman called Mac had imbibed began to increase his naturally mirthful tendencies. He threw back his head and howled. Bill eyed the narrator, who proceeded:

"It went on like that all winter, till the next spring. November the bunches of grass was five feet apart, December twenty feet, January nigh onto a quarter of a mile. It was curious. Cattle begun to be raised for speed. Them as could trot like the devil had it all their own way. They 'd light out of a mornin' and spin across the prairie, nippin' as they went, and finally git a full meal. Them as could n't, died. 'Long in the winter even trottin' would n't do. A steer had to eat on the dead run. They got to be a new kind of cattle introduced — racin' stock, lanky and lean-like. All around they was holdin' fairs and dealin' in cattle on a basis of speed. That there steer that could start out in the early mornin' in Wyoming and pull up with a full meal in Texas at night, — that there steer was the one that was worth the money. Then the next night he 'd come thunderin' back."

Petie stopped and clasped his chin with his hand and smiled complacently from the stool upon the company.

"What 's the little idiot talkin' about ?" said he of the whiskers, turning in his chair. "Do you fellers believe that ?"

"Every word of it," said Bill, solemnly. The liquor was making Mac take a more serious view of the story. He sat up, drinking in the details with a foolish look of cogitation on his face.

"Well, by this time they was all trained to gallop terrible."

"That 's good! that 's good!" said Mac, soberly; "gallop terrible."

"Why gentlemen," continued Petie, still holding his chin, "it was a matter o' necessary business to them steers."

"Which was?" said Jimmie, suddenly.

"The gallopin'. I 've stood out a many a mornin' and seen the prairie hot with 'em, like streaks o' lightnin' or shootin' stars, goin' every way. They knowed well enough it was their last day in this here world if they did n't. And sometimes they 'd git onto the same row o' grass goin' opposite ways, and meet and bust up in the middle. It was terrible. I could hear 'em bustin' up that way all along through the day."

"Petie," said Bill, shaking his head solemnly, "that sounds to me like a lie."

"It ain't, though, Bill—honest it ain't."

"Naw," said Mac, with a maudlin grin, "naw, Billy, it ain't."

Petie smiled and pointed with his thumb to him of the whiskers. Jimmie had sunk lower in his chair, with his hat resting on the bridge of his nose. They could hear his deep and regular breathing.

"She did n't rain, and it come spring and summer again, and finally August. The bunches was a mile apart, and then two miles, and then—"

"Lord, Petie," said Mac; "why, they could n't stand it—no siree. Nothin' could stand it. Somethin' 'd have to bust."

"You 're right. Somethin' did bust. It come oncet that there was n't but one bunch o' grass left in this here whole Western country. It happened of a Saturday afternoon. I was settin' on a high rock in the middle o' Colfax County, with the prairie all around as far as any man could see, and there was that little bunch o' grass out yonder 'bout a quarter of a mile. That mornin' every steer and cow and bull in New Mexico and Colorado— O, I reckon some from Wyoming and Arizona and Texas—maybe Utah, had got up and shook himself and looked out across the prairie towards Colfax County, and kind o' rose up on his toes and stretched himself out and felt of his muscles, and drawed in a deep breath and just lit out.

Everywheres they was comin'—stretched out—tails straight and vibratin'.

"Well, 'long about two o'clock I was settin' up on this here rock —"

"What was you doin' there, Petie?" said Bill.

"Thinkin'."

"But there was n't nothin' nowheres in sight, was there?"

"Nothin' but that there bunch o' grass, and just this here one rock, and sand all out everywheres."

"Let him alone, Bill, let him alone. He 's tellin' it like it was. Lord, do n't put in."

"But what was you doin' there, Petie?"

"Just thinkin', Bill, thinkin'. Perty soon come a kind of a breeze and blowed my hat off. I was considerin' gittin' it when I heard just a low hum, you know, all around. I looked up and I seen it was a little misty away off everywhere, but I did n't think much. But it kept on kind o' hummin', you know, and got louder and real deep. And first thing I knowed I seen 'em. I did n't know what they was,

Bill, for it was just a dark ring all round the horizon, gittin' bigger. It was roarin' now terrible, and comin' on and loomin' up. Then I knowed 'em. I could recognize particular bellers amongst 'em."

"Was n't they mashin' each other up, Petie?"

"Yes, Mac, they was that. Just mashin' 'em all up, gittin' so close, you know. Why, it was a wall o' steers comin'. Worse 'n thunder, too. I seen how it would end, for they was furious and pushed on, and I stood up. This here rock cut a big swath clean through 'em, for they was solid long before I seen 'em. Then perty soon they come together."

"Loud noise?"

"Loud noise, Bill."

"Must 'a' been bloody?"

"Nothin' but blood."

"Kill 'em?"

"Every one of 'em."

"How many was they?"

"'Bout a million—piled up terrible. A friend o' mine says he was in Denver then, and the air durin' Sunday and a part o' Monday was foggy and red."

" Blood ? "

" Sure. It was rainin' it down here. Rattle 'em up, Scaps, rattle 'em up ! "

The rattling of them up awoke him of the whiskers. When they had all drunk, Petie opened the door, turned about with his hand on his chin, gave them a parting smile, and disappeared. Jimmy stiffly arose and prepared to go. He too opened the door and paused. He turned with a look of unspeakable contempt on his be-whiskered face.

" You fellers could n't tell that was a lie ! " he said, and slammed the door behind him

THE ABSENCE OF NAR-CISSO

✦

ALL the long afternoon the Mexican bridal party had sat at the feast in the adobe house across the stream from the adobe fort. Felipa, the haughty Felipa, with her head proudly erect and her dark eyes wandering from the table to the door and from the door to the table, had sighed many times. Basilio, with whom she had stood before the altar in Cimarron in the early morning,—Basilio had rattled on in much cheap and aimless talk, and was smiling weakly. Basilio was a small man with a round and originally guileless face, like the face of a cherub. But one could surmise that the cherub's morals had drifted, for his eye had acquired an expression of cunning, and his lips betokened weakness of a complicated sort.

Viviana, the Maid of Honor, sat alone

234

beside Felipa. She was a little black-eyed Spanish girl, with a great deal of swift color coming and going in her cheeks, and her eyes restless. There was something in Viviana's manner indicating suppressed wrath. It added to her beauty. She talked much, however, and kept her feelings to herself. Beside Basilio sat the Gentleman of Honor, a broad, fierce, silent Mexican, named Pinto. It was four o'clock.

"Another glass with me, Señor Macready—now, now—one other glass with me!" said Viviana, puckering up her lips in the archest of smiling entreaties, and holding the tiny goblet aloft.

Señor Macready, the only guest at present at the table, sat opposite. He was a tall cowboy, very quiet and precise in his manner, which had something of reserve in it. He was fair, with high cheek-bones, very thin lips, and still blue eyes.

"Enough, Señorita; I have had enough," he replied, calmly surveying her face.

"No, no. Once more for me, Señor —for Viviana!"

" Once more, then, for Viviana."

Felipa, the bride, swept her haughty eyes slowly from the door to Macready's face. There was an odd spot of red high up in each cheek. Otherwise her face was darkly pale. As she spoke the spots of red throbbed just slightly.

" Señor Macready," she said in a low and melodious voice, speaking slowly, " what have you heard of the Señor Narcisso ? "

Viviana choked a little with the last swallow of her wine, which perhaps accounted for the quick rise of her color. Macready, passing two long fingers of one hand slowly up and down by the corners of his mouth, turned his blue eyes to the bride. Felipa met his gaze with her own dark ones.

" Narcisso ? Narcisso ? " broke in the weakly smiling Basilio, leaning over the table. " Why, that is so. Where in the world is he ? Narcisso ought to have come. Dear me ! Why, I 'm an old friend of Narcisso's."

" I 'm sure I don't know, Señora," said Macready slowly, dropping his eyes and

fingering a small cake by his plate. The
Señora was looking away at the door.

"O these fickle, these fickle friends!"
broke in Viviana, reviving from the chok-
ing, and putting unusual vehemence into
the adjective. "You men—you men! I
have half a mind to hate, to despise, every
one of you!" She smiled a swift smile
at Macready as she spoke.

"The men?" said Felipa's low voice
slowly. She poured out just a drop or
two of wine into a glass, and one might
have imagined there was a touch of sarcasm in her tone, a touch augmented by
the poise of her head. "The men? No,
Viviana; ah, no. The men are as true,
as true as the mountains, Viviana."

"The Señora," said Macready, not looking up, "is no doubt in a position to
know."

"The Gentleman of Honor over there,"
cried the sprightly Viviana, "is n't. He
is n't true to anything but the bottles. See
here, Señor Pinto, you are too abominably
quiet for anything. I just simply won't
have it, and that's all there is about it.
You big, fierce man!" smiling wickedly.

" You have n't said a thing for three solid
hours. What are you thinking about? "

The Gentleman of Honor had also
been staring at the door. He heaved a
deep sigh.

"Narcisso," he replied in a voice so
deep it seemed to shake the earthen floor.
" You happened to refer to Narcisso,
Señora Felipa. Yes, yes. I was thinking of Narcisso."

" Old friend of mine," broke in Basilio,
" old friend of mine. And Pinto, he 's
an old friend of mine. I 've got more
friends, ladies and gentlemen—I 've got
more friends than anything else in the
world. And Macready, he 's an old friend
of mine." Basilio grinned at the company.

" Do n't drink any more," said Felipa
decisively, with the faintest turn of her
shoulder away from Basilio.

" Narcisso—Narcisso," said Macready
quietly, as though to himself, and looking
at Felipa. " Yes, I wonder why he
did n't come to the feast? "

" Got into some trouble, I say," was
Pinto's deep bass reply. " Ha, ha! " he

laughed hoarsely; " he 's the very devil of a man, Narcisso."

"*Of* course, gentlemen, *of* course. Got into some trouble," said Basilio.

The musicians in the corner, an ancient Indian and a Mexican, with a fiddle and a guitar, having been for some time silent, struck up a Spanish air. As they did so, Felipa, who was again watching the door, gave a hardly noticeable start. There entered and approached the table another guest, brushing the dust of the prairies from his shoulders as he came.

He was a small, lithe Mexican, slender and graceful, with many a little swing to his gait and a manner affable in the extreme. In spite of an exceeding restless brilliancy of small black eye and the sweetest of affable smiles, there was something old-looking about his young face. He was of a strange pallor of countenance, sickly looking, with drawn lines about the smiling mouth. Like none other of the men present, he wore the velvet jacket and wide-flapping, gaudy trousers of the Spanish caballero.

" Ho, ho ! Montoya ! " thundered the deep-voiced Pinto in fiercely cordial greeting, getting up and placing a chair for the newcomer beside Macready. "Sit down! sit down!" The table shook under Pinto's great hand as he rested it upon it.

"Ah," said the smiling Montoya, standing by the table and bowing low to the ladies, with his hand over his heart. "Ah — delighted, delighted! The beautiful, the beautiful Señora Felipa — fairer than the flowers — lovely as the day! And my old friend, Basilio. Happiness, happiness, happiness! *And* the Maid of Honor — fair Señorita Viviana, ravishing Viviana — ah! *And* the Gentleman of Honor — ah! A day to be remembered forever. And the gentleman here; Señor, it seems I met you once. I remember. Macready, is it not? Macready."

With many a delicate curve of his fingers and his hands and his little old-young body, the affable Señor Montoya took his seat.

"We have just been pining away miserably, miserably, Señor Montoya," cried Viviana, puckering up her lips, "because you were not here!"

" Ah, the little flirt — the exquisite actress! My path lay over the prairies, fair one, flower of the field — over the barren sands. A traveler, you know; always a traveler ! "

" Did you — did you meet any one on the barren sands, señor ? " inquired Felipa, holding a glass in mid-air and bending her eyes on the little Mexican.

" Meet any one ? Ha, ha ! now let me see. Three Indians ! Who, now, Señora ? "

" She means old friends of ours — any old friends of ours," said Basilio. " Got lots of friends — every place you know. Day for good friends, you know, wedding-day. Montoya now, he 's an old friend of mine. All of you old friends of mine. Want you all to be good friends, you know. Eh, Montoya ? "

" There was one of them we were talking about a moment ago," said the Gentleman of Honor, swelling out his great chest and leaning back. " Friend of Basilio's. Narcisso."

Macready turned his blue eyes to Montoya's face. Viviana sipped wine with the pulses beating in her temples. Basilio smiled weakly about. Felipa, with her white face all the more emphasizing the two bright spots in her cheeks, held her proud head aloft and fastened her eyes on Montoya.

Montoya lifted a glass of wine in his small hand, eyed the liquor carefully, smiled sweetly upon the company, and said :

"Narcisso ? Ah — my old friend Narcisso. Has he not come ? I would have thought, fair ones, nothing beneath the stars could have kept him away ! Delayed, no doubt, señora, no doubt delayed."

"No doubt," said Macready quietly, with the faintest suggestion of disdain on his thin lips as he smiled back at Montoya. "And you, señor, you too were delayed ? "

Macready was watching Felipa's face, though his smile merged placidly into an expression of repose.

"It is true, Señor Montoya," inquired the bride, with some suggestion of coldness in her well-modulated tones, "that you too were delayed ?"

"Montoya is a flirt !" cried Viviana with passion. "Delayed ? What was she like, and what was the color of her eyes, and what did her lips look like?" Some of the suppressed wrath was apparent as she spoke.

"The little actress now!" ejaculated the smiling Montoya. "The color of her eyes? Fair one, they were as black as night and as bright as the stars and as deep as the sea! Her lips, flower of the field? Rich as the perfumes of Spain. Like? Fair one, she is like the angels with the harps; flower of the field, like you, exactly like you. And she led me here, Señorita, as fast as the prairies could travel beneath me!"

Macready was smiling reservedly to himself and still watching the bride. Having sipped a little more wine and addressed a ceremonious remark to the cherubic Basilio, he arose, bowed to the ladies, took his tall form to the door, and withdrew.

Other guests straggled in at intervals, and Montoya nibbled delicately at cakes and sipped his liquor and kept up his stream of lavish sociability. Felipa's eyes were upon him constantly. A little of the sarcasm hovered about her lips.

" Adios, fair ones—till the dance to-night," said Montoya, arising at last and bending his body in a low bow. " I must walk into the air, down the stream, to relax the strain of a traveler, you know. Maid of Honor, may I be dismissed for a stroll down the stream ? "

When he had gone Viviana twisted her forehead into many wrinkles.

" I have a very bad headache," she said miserably.

" You are sitting too long. Go out and walk," said Felipa.

" O, but it is n't the custom ! "

" Never mind the custom. We—we would n't have you suffer, you know."

" All good friends, you know—all good friends. Why, we 'll let you go," said Basilio. " And Pinto, the Gentleman of Honor — he 's a good friend of yours. He 'll excuse you."

" Well now," said the Gentleman of Honor in an amiable growl, " I 'll go with her. Come on, Maid of Honor; it is n't the custom, but it 's uncommonly comfortable."

With one hand to her forehead, the

other on the huge arm of the Gentleman
of Honor, and a pitiable expression of
much nervous weariness on her face, Viviana withdrew.

The headache having brought her and
her companion among the low willows to
a great bowlder several hundred yards down
the stream, it led them to the other side
of it. Señor Montoya was sitting there
by the water's edge looking pensively at
the ripples. The Maid of Honor lost no
time in breaking into a passion and stamp-
ing her small foot with great vehemence.

"This is a pretty end of it!" she cried.
"This is a beautiful—oh, a beautiful end
of it! What in the world is the matter
with you all?"

"Now, now," said the affable Montoya,
his affability wearing something of haggardness, "do n't let the Señorita get carried away with herself. Be more quiet.
Let the Maid of Honor be more calm!"

The huge Pinto leaned against the rock
with an ill expression of countenance, and
let the Maid of Honor fight it out.

"But where is Narcisso, and where are
the horses, and the firing of pistols, and

the tearing away — and all the beautiful
plan ? " The Señorita's face showed all
varieties of Spanish color.

" Coming, my dear, coming."

" Coming ? " to the last degree exaspe-
rated. " Coming! Well, the heavens help
us, what good are they going to do now? "

" Carry her away, my beloved ; what
else do you want ? "

" And married already ! "

" Now, you pretty little flower of the
field, what difference is it to Narcisso ?
Never will it bother his head. Married ?
Ha, ha ! — why, bless your sweet cheeks,
I was one time married myself. For thirty-
three minutes, Señorita ! "

" Do you mean to tell me, you little
rascal, you deceiver—do you mean to tell
me that Narcisso is coming yet ? "

" To-night, flower of the field."

" You are lying to me ! "

" You are beautiful in a passion, fair
one. If you were to put your little ear
to the ground, you would hear the tread of
his charger's feet."

" But what will he do when he gets
here ? I do n't believe it ! "

" There, there, little one; you go running away with yourself. Do? Dios!
beloved, what do you expect him to do?
Narcisso will carry off the bride — what
else? And I — I, most beautiful Señorita,
Maid of Honor, just as the plans were
laid long ago — I will carry you off!"

" This is a mess!" broke in the deep
voice of Pinto, as he looked fiercely at
Montoya. " This is a sweet mess!"

" A mess, Señor?" replied Montoya,
the lines about his mouth drawn a little
more, perhaps. " What difference is it
to you, Señor? You will get your money,
my excellent friend. Your services are
good, my excellent friend."

Montoya was sitting eyeing the Maid
of Honor, with a smile of much sweetness
playing over his features, and the angry
Viviana was on the point of breaking
forth once more, when Macready walked
leisurely round the corner of the rock.
He was alternately stretching and relaxing
his thin lips over his teeth, and deftly
rolling a cigarette in his long fingers. His
blue eyes rested placidly on the tobacco.
Viviana started back against the rock.

"Ah," said Montoya, the smile being abated; "you have listened, Señor? Cowards listen, Señor."

"What in the devil are you prowling around here for?" thundered the bristling Pinto.

Macready quietly finished rolling his cigarette and lighted it. When he was puffing smoke into the air, he turned his eyes on Montoya.

"I am ready, Señor," he said, "to hear the rest of it, now."

Viviana was holding her breath, the color coming and going in her cheeks. Montoya's black eyes stared at Macready.

"Which side are you on, Señor Macready?"

"Either side," said Macready, with a reserved laugh. He turned to Viviana. "The Maid of Honor," he said, with a touch of sarcasm. "I can say, Señors and Señorita, I had at one time imagined I had some feeling for the Maid of Honor." He quietly took his cigarette from his lips and pushed the ashes from it with his little finger. "But," he continued, smiling slightly, "I imagine it no more. For Basilio I have perhaps

some little feeling. And, by the way,—"
he puffed a little at the cigarette and
rubbed his fingers up and down the corners
of his mouth,—" I should like—it would
give me pleasure to stop the Señorita."

Montoya sat long in silence, watching
the cowboy and meditating. Finally he
seemed to have come to a conclusion.

" Come with me," he said to Macready.
" Come! Down the stream here; we talk
about it. You go on that way. I will
say a thing to the Señorita." Macready
sauntered down the stream.

" This is beautiful now, is n't it?" cried
Viviana.

" A devil of a mess!" growled Pinto.

" Hush, beautiful one," whispered the
smiling Montoya, bending in a low bow
to the Señorita, speaking rapidly and with
much elegance of expression. " Come;
go back to the bride. Tell her that we
have had a very great accident on the
road, which kept the Señor Narcisso till
night, when he would have been here
early in the morning. Tell her I, Montoya, greet her as ambassador, minister—
ha, ha!—minister of every kind of affairs

from Narcisso, and that he is coming—
coming, you hear? And tell her—hist!—
tell her that the fact that she is not any
more the Señorita, that she is the Señora
of my dear friend Basilio—hist!—it makes
not any damn difference! Go with her,
Pinto; go back. They will notice. I will
attend to this gentleman of the long fingers,
fair one. Go, flower of the field, go!"

Pinto and the Maid of Honor departed,
and, smiling sweetly, Montoya followed
the tall cowboy, and took his arm with
much graciousness.

"Señor," he said, "keep yourself calm.
Hist!—it is a lie!"

"Ah," said Macready, "which—which
part?"

"Basilio's wedding."

"A lie, eh?"

"We arranged it very long before, Basilio and I. These people do not know it,
the Gentleman and the Maid of Honor. I
might as well tell you, for you are the
good friend of my old friend Basilio. No
wedding, no license, no justice. We have
a man in Cimarron to say the words—a
cowboy like you, Señor."

" Well, what is it for? "

" Hist! Felipa's father makes her marry Basilio. If not, she gets no five hundred dollars, which he will give to Basilio. He thinks there is nobody like Basilio. Hist! Basilio and Felipa have me to arrange the wedding, and I fix up the lie. Then we three divide the money. They come driving, driving home, and Narcisso, cowboys with him, horses, pistols—whist!—takes the girl! Now listen, Señor." He was watching Macready's face with much intensity. " There has been a mistake. There is delay. An accident keeps Narcisso away so that he cannot come till to-night. But he will come. So, you see, Basilio is not any poor fool."

" Hm," said Macready, " glad you told me all that. Very interesting. With his cowboys, eh? I have a number of cowboys myself— horses — pistols. Señor Montoya, I am not particularly pleased. I still think, Señor, that even if Basilio is not any poor fool," he knocked the ashes from his cigarette—" I should like to stop the Señorita."

Montoya's restless eyes were shifting

from the face of Macready to the stream
and back again. He was silent for some
time, apparently thinking with intense ra-
pidity.

"Señor," he said at last.

"What is it now?"

"There is another lie, too."

"Hm—only one more?"

"It is this, Señor—Hist! Narcisso is
not coming!" His keen eyes were on
Macready's face.

Macready puffed and returned the gaze.

"No," continued Montoya, speaking
quickly, the haggard look about the mouth
more plainly defined. "Observe. Felipa
is deceived."

"Is any one coming for her, then?"

"Quien sabe, Señor? quien sabe? Hist!
—be not so afraid I will run away with
the Maid of Honor. Maybe—I do not
know, but maybe—she is stopped already.
Perhaps I am not so madly in love with
the Señorita. Leave it to me, Señor, leave
it to me!"

"Then where is Narcisso?"

"Delayed, Señor, delayed."

"I will say this much and go," said

Macready. "Lies, eh? Yes, I should judge so. There is no possible way of believing you, Señor, so I believe nothing. I wait and see. You may be right, but, observe, Señor Montoya, I will be ready. I, too, have cowboys. Several can be in the same trouble. Adios, my friend—*A mas ver!*" Macready cast his cigarette into the stream and went back to the fort.

At half-past seven the bridal procession had wound its way from the house of the feast, across the stream, to the adobe dance-hall by the fort. There were many cowboys about, both without and within, and much saddling of horses in the dusk. The dance-hall was small, and there was nothing in it save a few lamps and low wooden benches about the wall, and at one end a very high stool for the master of the dances. The walls and floor were earthern. A Spanish dance was struck up and the festivities began.

"With the beautiful Señorita, Maid of Honor, beauty of Spain, I shall have the first dance!" cried Montoya. "Come away, fair one, flower of the field!"

" O, Señor, the custom, Señor! I dance first with the Gentleman of Honor."

" Custom? Bah! not any. Ha, ha! The Gentleman of Honor will excuse the beautiful, the Señorita—for a traveler? "

The Gentleman of Honor, with an air of great grandeur, waved the two aside and excused the Señorita. The little Mexican whirled away with her. With little grace and but passive enjoyment the cherub swung the bride away. The tall Macready carried, as it were, a little hybrid girl about. The numerous friends and relatives found themselves partners and joined in. Fiddle and guitar ran an unbridled race, with the old Indian beating his heavy foot rythmically upon the floor.

Montoya's eyes were brilliantly restless. His small visage wore the customary pallor of his bloodless skin; something like haggardness again hovered about the mouth. But there was the same smile still.

" The dance! the dance! the dance! " he cried in the middle of it, swinging his body into exquisite curves and gliding back and forth and up and down among

the moving company with the blushing
Señorita. " Beloved, I am carried away !
Ah, the Señor Macready — calm as ever,
tall as ever, superior Macready! Basilio
— my old friend Basilio ! And the Señora,
the beautiful Señora ! "

The second dance was a waltz. Before
it Macready observed Felipa standing in
the corner with Montoya before her, the
latter talking rapidly. Felipa's face was
whiter still, and the lips were pressed
tightly together. The small red spots on
her cheeks were brilliant. Macready was
struck with a certain look of daring that
had come over her face.

" Heavens ! " he said to himself, " look
at that girl ! Like a panther. She 's ready
for anything."

He approached her. Her eyes seemed
unusually wide. They were slowly sweeping the company and the three small windows as she listened to Montoya.

" Let me have the waltz ? " said Macready.

" Ah," cried the smiling Montoya,
breaking in suddenly, " just asking for it
myself. Beg a thousand pardons, Señor,

but I could n't give her up — the fair
Señora ! "

A look of some disdain came over
Felipa's features. She smiled slightly to
Macready.

" You must excuse me," she said.

" Certainly," replied Macready, calmly
walking away.

" You should dance with the Gentleman of Honor next, Señora," growled
Pinto, coming up. " The custom, you
know."

" Ah — custom, custom ! what is it ?
The Gentleman of Honor will excuse a
traveler — just for the once ! "

The dance was already beginning, and
Montoya, with his arm about the bride,
waltzed away.

" He 's carrying things mighty high,"
growled Pinto fiercely, —" mighty high ! "

To rid his huge body of the heat of the
room Pinto stepped outside the door. The
breath of the night fanned his face. Beneath the shadow of some willows at a
distance down the stream a shifting of
vague forms might have told of horses
saddled and cowboys lying by the water.

Under the stars the silent plain stretched miles and miles away between the mesas, and straight down the middle of it lay the trail that led into the desert.

Montoya was still waltzing with the bride. Basilio's arm encircled the delicate waist of the Maid of Honor. Macready and the other cowboys and Mexicans were gliding about, Macready's calm gaze constantly following Montoya. The little Mexican's eyes were shifting quickly from those of Felipa to the three windows. His smile was there as always, but he was talking in a low tone.

" Ah, Señora ! to be with thee ! "

" I insist that you cease to talk to me so, Señor," she replied haughtily; " and tell me when, in the name of Heaven, he is coming. I will not stand this much longer."

" Have patience, my love, have patience. The noble, the excellent Narcisso lets nothing stop him. He is coming."

" Montoya, there is something wrong in this—it is n't going right. Some of us will be killed."

" Patience, beloved. Killed ? Ha ! Who cares, Señora ? No, no. Not Narcisso." There was a strange light in his eyes as he fastened them on her and smiled. " And who would not risk it—for these, these eyes ? Ah, Señora, who would not risk it ! And the cheek, Señora, and the lips—ah, the ravishing lips ! Dios ! it would make any man mad—mad ! Hist ! Señora; I could swing you away—*myself!*" The deftness of speech was not abated, nor the air of affability ; but the eyes on hers were glittering. The Señora loosened herself a little in his clasp and looked at him scornfully.

" How is he going to get me away—tell me quick ! I must be ready. Señor Montoya, I hate your eyes ! Look at me no more. I think, Señor, you lie ! "

" And the color of the forehead—maddening ! And the delicate form, and the dainty feet ! Señora, you are beautiful as no one else is beautiful ! "

The waltz was taking a slightly faster turn, and the fiddle and the guitar were beating away in swifter rhythm. The lights danced before Felipa's eyes. Montoya's colorless face was close to hers. She could not free herself.

" Listen, Señora ; I am a wanderer ; the night is my home—the mountains are my friends—the stars are my people. Señora, I am alone ! I am mad with it, the being alone. Hist ! I see these eyes, the cheek, the lips, the forehead, the hair, —ah, Señora, I become in a fever. The night, the mountains, the stars—they are hell ! Beautiful one—I, Montoya, the traveler—I love you ! "

The girl caught her breath in a gasp, and tried to wrench from his arms, but he held her. He was still smiling and speaking under his breath.

" No, no—do not go away yet, Señora. What if I tell you I can take you away as well as Narcisso ? Listen, Señora—*better* than Narcisso ! "

" Then he is not coming ! " cried the girl. " You liar ! you fiend ! He is not coming ! "

" The bright, the intelligent Felipa. Ah, a mind like the face—beautiful, beauful ! The time is here—the horses are coming ; hist ! the guns ! But as for Narcisso, Señora —"

With a quick scream Felipa tore herself

from him, darted across to the opposite
wall, and stood defiantly with her back
against it, her eyes flashing. The dancers
stopped in sudden confusion, and the fiddle
and the guitar broke abruptly off. Montoya stood in the center of the room, meet-
ing the general gaze with the affable smile,
his eyes shining. There was a second's
intense silence. The next instant the
sound of galloping hoofs echoed upon the
prairie trail, and Pinto's great form burst
into the door.

"Narcisso!" he yelled in a voice of
thunder. "Ready, men! It is Narcisso!"

With a shout Montoya's lithe figure
leaped toward the Señora. He had
whipped out a revolver, and, pointing it at
the ceiling, fired three shots, as a signal,
through the roof. Pinto seized the tall
stool and with one blow dashed it in pieces
against the wall. In a second he was
armed with one of its legs, and, swinging
it about his head, dashed for the door.

But Macready and three others were too
quick for the Mexicans. Montoya, with
his arm about the girl's waist and almost
carrying her, was already stopped short.

Pinto was brought up by a powerful blow upon the head from Macready's fist, before his club had had time to execute its work. Most of the men took sides immediately, the women huddling together at the far side of the room. In a moment more there would have been a general fight.

"Stop! Stop!" cried the Señora. Exerting all her strength, she wrenched herself once again from the arms of Montoya, and, darting to the center of the room, stood like a tigress at bay. "Hold the door! Keep Montoya! I will not go one step! The fiend! Well done, Señor Macready! All of you cowards, come on! Bar the door! Down with them—down with them!"

The galloping of horses had ceased, and there was a great shout without. The three small windows were suddenly broken in with a crash. Montoya turned about, and was starting for one of these new openings, when the great Gentleman of Honor, quickly comprehending the new turn affairs had taken, a turn which Macready himself was just beginning to understand, caught the little Mexican from behind with his long arms and swiftly pinioned him against the wall; the bewildered Maid of Honor, in a passion, meanwhile doing her best, with teeth and nails, to loosen his grip.

Macready and the cowboys immediately leaped to the windows, such as had no weapons arming themselves with the fragments of the stool. The heads of several who would have entered from without received blows of no indecisive force. A scramble ensued at each window. Macready was leaning far out of one, struggling with some unseen opponent. At this moment there was a counter-rush of horses' feet on the trail, a short scuffle, many curses and random shots, and a dashing retreat.

The cherubic Basilio stood nerveless against the wall, a pitiable smile on his weak features. Macready turned calmly about and cast his blue eyes over the company. The disgraceful scene having arrived at something of a standstill, the Maid of Honor ceased her attacks upon the now violently enangered Pinto, and the Gentleman of Honor, weary of the struggle, let the desperate Montoya loose. Felipa, her great eyes dilating, was standing, white and silent, against the wall.

Montoya stepped calmly to the center of the room, deftly brushed the dust of the wall from his velvet jacket, and swept the company slowly with his eyes. His face was a little more drawn and the eyes a little more glittering; but as he gazed about, the sweet, sweet smile broke over his pallid features.

" Ah," he said, bowing gracefully. " It was very excellently done. Señora, it was beautiful, beautiful. And the Señor Macready—wonderful! You all have it so well made up. *And* the Gentleman of Honor—ah! *And* the Maid of Honor—ah! There is just one thing I should like to say. You will let me step to the door—a traveler, you know; here by the door? I will do some talking now."

They would have stopped him, but Macready interfered.

" Let him go, let him go," said the cowboy. " You can't do anything."

" Ah, thank you, Señor—thank you. I only go just here, Señor, to the door, till

I have said something. Now, look you, all of you. Narcisso did not get the girl— ah, no; and why? Because, Señors— look at her there, the beautiful Señora, the daring Señora—because I, Montoya, love her myself! Is Montoya into this affair, my friends, for his health? Is he carrying away the beautiful Señora for somebody else? Not at all, Señors. Hist! Where is Narcisso? Look you—I *hate* Narcisso! I think, shall he have the beautiful one? No, no. I show you now, before I go, that I am not so much a fool. I show you, too, flower of the field, Maid of Honor, that you are not for me. I show you, too, Señora, the beautiful, the beloved Señora, that if I do not have you myself, I see that nobody else has you. Do not look for Narcisso. Do not look for Ba- silio. You yourself know, and you may tell it to the company when I have gone, why my old friend Basilio is no husband of yours. I, too, know it, Señora, for I am the excellent confidant of Basilio. But look you, daring one, you thought that I, Montoya, was working for the money. A curse upon the money, Señora — no,

Señorita!—a curse upon the money! Who was it made my excellent friend Basilio turn away from the fair Felipa and take the money instead? I, I, Montoya. And as for Narcisso; look you, my friends, he had me to carry away the beautiful one for him. But before I came— "—he was caressing the revolver and holding it ready and backing nearer to the door—" before I came, Señors, I arranged it with Narcisso. You will find him away, away, beneath the stars—away on the desert sands. It was for her who stands there so beautiful, so daring now. The night was still, the coyotes were crying over the mesas, the moon was dead. And so, Señors, remember this of Montoya—he killed Narcisso. I have not yet the girl; but never mind; another time, perhaps. *A mas ver*, Señor Macready. You are of deep mind. Beloved one, beautiful Felipa, *Adios!* Farewell, flower of the field, farewell!"

Before they had understood his meaning or come from under the control of his shining eyes, he was gone, and a second later the gallop of his horse's feet echoed away into the night.

PRINTED AT THE LAKESIDE
PRESS FOR H. S. STONE & CO.
PUBLISHERS, CHICAGO

CATALOGUE · OF · BOOKS · IN · BELLES · LETTRES

Chicago   New York

MDCCCXCVII

MESSRS. HERBERT S. STONE & COMPANY TAKE PLEASURE IN ANNOUNCING THE FOLLOWING PUBLICATIONS AS IN PREPARATION:

The next novel by Harold Frederic,
　　Author of "The Damnation of Theron Ware."

"Dross," a novel by Henry Seton Merriman.
　　Author of "The Sowers," etc.

And new books by George Ade, author of
　　"Artie," and Henry M. Blossom, Jr.,
　　Author of "Checkers."

　　Further particulars will be given later.

LONDON OFFICE: 10 NORFOLK ST., STRAND.
CABLE ADDRESSES:
"CHAPBOOK, CHICAGO."
"CHAPBOOK, NEW YORK."
"EDITORSHIP, LONDON."

THE PUBLICATIONS OF HERBERT S. STONE & CO. THE CHAP-BOOK

CAXTON BUILDING, CHICAGO
111 FIFTH AVENUE, NEW YORK

Ade, George.

> ARTIE: *A Story of the Streets and of the Town. With many pictures by* JOHN T. McCUTCHEON. *16mo.* $1.25.
>
> *Ninth thousand.*

"Mr. Ade shows all the qualities of a successful novelist."—*Chicago Tribune.*

"Artie is a character, and George Ade has limned him deftly as well as amusingly. Under his rollicking abandon and recklessness we are made to feel the real sense and sensitiveness, and the worldly wisdom of a youth whose only language is that of a street-gamin. As a study of the peculiar type chosen, it is both typical and inimitable."—*Detroit Free Press.*

"It is brimful of fun and picturesque slang. Nobody will be any the worse for reading about Artie, if he does talk slang. He's a good fellow at heart, and Mamie Carroll is the 'making of him.' He talks good sense and good morality, and these things have n't yet gone out of style, even in Chicago."—*New York Recorder.*

"Well-meaning admirers have compared Artie

3

to Chimmie Fadden, but Mr. Townsend's creation, excellent as it is, cannot be said to be entirely free from exaggeration. The hand of Chimmie Fadden's maker is to be discerned at times. And just here Artie is particularly strong—he is always Artie, and Mr. Ade is always concealed, and never obtrudes his personality."—*Chicago Post.*

"George Ade is a writer, the direct antithesis of Stephen Crane. In 'Artie' he has given the world a story of the streets at once wholesome, free, and stimulating. The world is filled with people like 'Artie' Blanchard and his 'girl,' 'Mamie' Carroll, and the story of their lives, their hopes, and dreams, and loves, is immeasurably more wholesome than all the stories like 'George's Mother' that could be written by an army of the writers who call themselves realists."—Editorial *Albany Evening Journal.*

Benham, Charles.

THE FOURTH NAPOLEON: *A Romance.* *12mo.* $1.50.

An accurate account of the history of the Fourth Napoleon, the *coup d'état* which places him on the throne of France, the war with Germany, and his love intrigues as emperor. A vivid picture of contemporary politics in Paris.

Blossom, Henry M., Jr.

CHECKERS: *A Hard-Luck Story. By the author of* "*The Documents in Evidence.*" *16mo.* $1.25. *Seventh edition.*

"Abounds in the most racy and picturesque slang."—*New York Recorder.*

"'Checkers' is an interesting and entertaining

chap, a distinct type, with a separate tongue and a way of saying things that is oddly humorous."—*Chicago Record.*

"If I had to ride from New York to Chicago on a slow train, I should like a half-dozen books as gladsome as 'Checkers,' and I could laugh at the trip."—*New York Commercial Advertiser.*

"'Checkers' himself is as distinct a creation as Chimmie Fadden, and his racy slang expresses a livelier wit. The racing part is clever reporting, and as horsey and 'up to date' as any one could ask. The slang of the racecourse is caught with skill and is vivid and picturesque, and students of the byways of language may find some new gems of colloquial speech to add to their lexicons."—*Springfield Republican.*

Chap-Book Essays.

A VOLUME OF REPRINTS FROM THE CHAP-BOOK. *Contributions by* T. W. HIGGINSON, H. W. MABIE, LOUISE CHANDLER MOULTON, H. H. BOYESEN, EDMUND GOSSE, JOHN BURROUGHS, NORMAN HAPGOOD, MRS. REGINALD DE KOVEN, LOUISE IMOGEN GUINEY, LEWIS E. GATES, ALICE MORSE EARLE, LAURENCE JERROLD, RICHARD HENRY STODDARD, EVE BLANTYRE SIMPSON, *and* MAURICE THOMPSON, *with a cover designed by* A. E. BORIE. *16mo.* $1.25.

Chap-Book Stories.

A VOLUME OF REPRINTS FROM THE CHAP-BOOK. *Contributions by* OCTAVE THANET, GRACE ELLERY CHANNING, MARIA LOUISE POOL, *and Others. 16mo.* $1.25. *Second edition.*

The authors of this volume are all American. Besides the well-known names, there are some which were seen in the CHAP-BOOK for the first time. The volume is bound in an entirely new and startling fashion.

Chatfield-Taylor, H. C.

THE LAND OF THE CASTANET: *Spanish Sketches, with twenty-five full-page illustrations. 12mo.* $1.25.

"Gives the reader an insight into the life of Spain at the present time which he cannot get elsewhere."—*Cincinnati Commercial Tribune.*

"Mr. Chatfield-Taylor's word-painting of special events—the bull-fight, for instance—is vivid and well-colored. He gets at the national character very well indeed, and we feel that we know our Spain better by reason of his handsome little book."—*Boston Traveler.*

"He writes pleasantly and impartially, and very fairly sums up the Spanish character. . . . Mr. Taylor's book is well illustrated, and is more readable than the reminiscences of the average globe-trotter."—*New York Sun.*

D'Annunzio, Gabriele.

EPISCOPO AND COMPANY. *Translated by Myrta Leonora Jones. 16mo. $1.25.*
Second edition.

Gabriele d'Annunzio is the best-known and most gifted of modern Italian novelists. His work is making a great sensation at present in all literary circles. The translation now offered gives the first opportunity English-speaking readers have had to know him in their own language.

De Fontenoy, The Marquise.

EVE'S GLOSSARY. *By the author of "Queer Sprigs of Gentility," with decorations in two colors by* FRANK HAZENPLUG. *4to.*
Nearly ready.

An amusing volume of gossip and advice for gentlewomen. It treats of health, costume, and entertainments; exemplifies by reference to noted beauties of England and the Continent; and is embellished with decorative borders of great charm.

Earle, Alice Morse.

CURIOUS PUNISHMENTS OF BYGONE DAYS, *with twelve quaint pictures and a cover design by* FRANK HAZENPLUG. *12mo. $1.50.*

" In this dainty little volume, Alice Morse Earle has done a real service, not only to present readers, but to future students of bygone customs. To come upon all the information that is here put into readable shape, one would be obliged to search

7

through many ancient and cumbrous records."—
Boston Transcript.

" Mrs. Alice Morse Earle has made a diverting
and edifying book in her 'Curious Punishments
of Bygone Days,' which is published in a style of
quaintness befitting the theme."—*New York
Tribune*

"This light and entertaining volume is the most
recent of Mrs. Earle's popular antiquarian sketches,
and will not fail to amuse and mildly instruct
readers who love to recall the grim furnishings and
habits of previous centuries, without too much
serious consideration of the root from which they
sprang, the circumstances in which they flour-
ished, or the uses they served."—*The Independent.*

Hichens, Robert.

FLAMES: *A novel. By the author of "A
Green Carnation," "An Imaginative
Man," "The Folly of Eustace," etc., with
a cover-design by* F. R. KIMBROUGH.
12mo. $1.50.

Mr. Hichens's reputation has steadily increased
since the brilliant success of " A Green Carnation" first gave him prominence. His latest work
is longer and more important than anything he
has done before.

James, Henry.

WHAT MAISIE KNEW: *A novel. 12mo.*
(*In preparation.*)

Upon its completion in the CHAP-BOOK, Mr.
Henry James's latest novel will be issued in book-
form. Its publication cannot fail to be an event

of no slight literary importance, and will be worthy the attention of all persons interested in English and American letters.

Kinross, Albert.

THE FEARSOME ISLAND ; *Being a modern rendering of the narrative of one Silas Fordred, Master Mariner of Hythe, whose shipwreck and subsequent adventures are herein set forth. Also an appendix, accounting in a rational manner for the seeming marvels that Silas Fordred encountered during his sojourn on the fearsome island of Don Diego Rodriguez. With a cover designed by* FRANK HAZENPLUG. *16mo.* $1.25.

Le Gallienne, Richard.

PROSE FANCIES: *Second series. By the author of* "*The Book-Bills of Narcissus,*" "*The Quest of the Golden Girl,*" *etc. With a cover designed by* FRANK HAZENPLUG. *16mo.* $12.5. *Second edition.*

"In these days of Beardsley pictures and decadent novels, it is good to find a book as sweet, as pure, as delicate as Mr. Le Gallienne's."—*New Orleans Picayune.*

"'Prose Fancies' ought to be in every one's summer library, for it is just the kind of a book one loves to take to some secluded spot to read and dream over."—*Kansas City Times.*

and a journalistic admirer are, in particular, absolute triumphs. The book is wonderfully witty, and has touches of genuine pathos, more than two and more than three. It is much better than anything else we **have seen** from the same hand."—*Pall Mall Gazette.*

"Lucas Malet has insight, strength, the gift of satire, and a captivating brilliance of touch; in short, a literary equipment such as not too many present-day novelists are possessed of."—*London Daily Mail.*

"We cannot think of readers as skipping a line or failing to admire the workmanship, or to be deeply interested, both in the characters and the plot. 'Carissima' is likely to add to the reputation of the author of 'The Wages of Sin.'"—*Glasgow Herald.*

Moore, F. Frankfort.

THE IMPUDENT COMEDIAN AND OTHERS. *Illustrated. 12mo.* $1.50.

Several of the stories have appeared in the CHAP-BOOK; others are now published for the first time. They all relate to seventeenth and eighteenth century characters—Nell Gwynn, Kitty Clive, Oliver Goldsmith, Dr. Johnson, and David Garrick. They are bright, witty, and dramatic.

THE JESSAMY BRIDE: *A Novel. By the author of "The Impudent Comedian." 12mo.* $1.50.

A novel of great interest, introducing as its chief characters Goldsmith, Johnson, Garrick, Sir Joshua Reynolds and others. It is really a companion volume to "The Impudent Comedian."

Morrison, Arthur.

A CHILD OF THE JAGO. *By the author of "Tales of Mean Streets." 12mo. $1.50. Second edition.*

***This, the first long story which Mr. Morrison has written, is, like his remarkable "Tales of Mean Streets," a realistic study of East End life.

"The power and art of the book are beyond question."—*Hartford Courant.*

"It is one of the most notable books of the year."—*Chicago Daily News.*

"'A Child of the Jago' will prove one of the immediate and great successes of the season."—*Boston Times.*

"Since Daniel Defoe, no such consummate master of realistic fiction has arisen among us as Mr. Arthur Morrison. Hardly any praise could be too much for the imaginative power and artistic perfection and beauty of this picture of the depraved and loathsome phases of human life. There is all of Defoe's fidelity of realistic detail, suffused with the light and warmth of a genius higher and purer than Defoe's."—*Scotsman.*

"It more than fulfills the promise of 'Tales of Mean Streets'—it makes you confident that Mr. Morrison has yet better work to do. The power displayed is magnificent, and the episode of the murder of Weech, 'fence' and 'nark,' and of the capture and trial of his murderer, is one that stamps itself upon the memory as a thing done once and for all. Perrott in the dock, or as he awaits the executioner, is a fit companion of Fagin condemned. The book cannot but confirm the admirers of Mr. Morrison's remarkable talent in the opinions they formed on reading 'Tales of Mean Streets.'"—*Black and White.*

www.ingramcontent.com/pod-product-compliance
Lightning Source LLC
Chambersburg PA
CBHW030632030726
47497CB00006B/1746